Knock and Enter

An Anthology from
Dublin City Libraries' Writing Groups

Edited by
Declan Burke

KNOCK AND ENTER

Published in 2021 by Dublin City Libraries

Editor: Declan Burke

ISBN 978-1-8384635-3-3

Designed and printed by Anglo Printers.

This Book was made possible through the financial assistance of the Department of Tourism, Culture, Arts, Gaeltacht, Sport and Media.

This first edition is dedicated to the memory of Orla Ní hAonigh who established and supported writing groups at Ballymun, Cabra and Kevin Street Libraries.

Orla was one of life's givers and is sadly missed by all who knew her.

Contents

Introduction

There has been a long and rich history of writing groups in Dublin City Libraries. People from different backgrounds with different levels of writing experience are welcomed into the open and democratic space of their local library where they receive support and feedback from their fellow writers.

With its designation as a UNESCO City of Literature, Dublin values writers of all abilities. And whether writing is a hobby or a pathway to a career, writing groups offer the space and encouragement to writers to develop their skills at their own pace.

I hope you enjoy reading the various pieces of poetry and prose in *Knock and Enter* and that the collection will be available to borrow from libraries around the country, inspiring other writing groups to produce their own collections.

I'd like to pay particular thanks to the author Declan Burke for his expertise and care in editing this collection. I know he really enjoyed working with the writing groups over the last few years and they in turn have benefitted from his experience and wisdom.

Mairead Owens
Dublin City Librarian

Foreword

I've always thought that the octopus would make for an ideal editor, with its eight arms and complex nervous system, which consists of one main brain and eight mini-brains that operate each arm independently.

Of course, most writers would likely also wish that their editors were octopuses, given that octopodes possess three hearts, one of which might be given over to compassion for those who toil at the coalface creating the imperishable prose and poetry which the editor, having nothing better to do, then proceeds to blithely deface with his or her 'suggestions' and 'advice'.

Happily, whilst all octopuses are venomous, only the blue-ringed octopus is actually deadly to humans; and while the business of writing can be a somewhat tiresome chore – planning and writing and editing, and rewriting, and re-editing, and then rewriting some more – it very rarely proves fatal.

This journal is a collection of prose, poetry and memoir contributed by participants in the creative writing groups attached to a variety of Dublin City Libraries, most of whom write, and then read their contributions aloud, for their peers on a weekly basis. Writing for posterity, of course, is a different beast entirely, and requires a more painstaking approach to the business of saying exactly what we mean and making that meaning crystal-clear to the future reader, who may pick the journal off the library shelf next week, or next year, or 20 years hence. It is in this context that we start to understand that that hoariest of literary clichés – writing *is* rewriting – possesses more than a kernel of truth. Stephen King, who knows a thing or two about putting words in their best order, says that he writes the first draft of a story for himself, and that all subsequent drafts are written for the reader. And yes, that's drafts plural.

I thoroughly enjoyed the experience of editing *Knock and Enter*, and not least because it has exposed me to a myriad of styles, themes and stories at an unprecedented time in our history. *Knock and Enter* was written and compiled against the backdrop of the Covid-19 pandemic, so it will come as no surprise that some of the offerings here are directly influenced by the lockdowns, the confusion, the grief and the social dislocation that has come in its wake. And yet, much of the response has been unexpected – blackly comic tales of emotional triumphs, surreal visions of alternate realities, quietly moving testimonies to the indestructibility of the human spirit.

The most pleasurable aspect of editing this journal, however, was engaging with writers who had little previous experience of being edited, many of whom had never been previously published, but who responded by engaging enthusiastically and whole-heartedly with the process. Seeing the stories and poems, and the writers themselves, begin to fulfil their promise was a hugely rewarding experience, and one that I hope the reader can appreciate.

The title of *Knock and Enter*, incidentally, is derived from a story submitted to a previous iteration of this journal, one that was stalled in its tracks, as so many endeavours were, when Covid-19 first appeared. Written by Oliver Nolan from the Donaghmede writing group, the story charts the tentative journey of a recent retiree who approaches a library-based creative writing group with trepidation, only to be warmly welcomed into the fold.

That title was chosen by Alison Lyons, former director of Dublin UNESCO City of Literature at Dublin City Council. As many of the literary innovations established by Dublin City Council tend to be, *Knock and Enter* is Alison's brainchild. I'd like to take the opportunity to thank Alison, Anne-Marie Kelly and Jackie Lynam, also of Dublin UNESCO City of Literature, for not only devising and greenlighting *Knock and Enter* but for their phenomenal support for the library-based creative writing groups.

I would also like to thank the writers themselves, without whom this journal would be a rather brief and pointless affair. Certain aspects of writing can be taught, of course, although it's been my experience as a creative writing teacher, and as the good Dr Johnson once suggested, that we need to be reminded more often that we need to be instructed; but the one thing that cannot be taught is the *instinct* to write, the inextinguishable spark that is required to create, and which, carefully tended and nurtured, results in publications such as *Knock and Enter*.

Reader, I hope you enjoy.

Declan Burke
June 2021

Summer Meline

Summer Meline has facilitated the Donaghmede Library Writers' Group since 2015. She holds an MPhil in Creative Writing from Trinity College and was a recipient of the inaugural Ireland Chair of Poetry Student Award. In 2020, she was a co-editor of the poetry anthology *Hold Open the Door*, published by UCD Press. She lives in Dublin with her husband, two children and a rescue cat.

Forager

All it takes is a simple taste for me
to remember our home, and I am moved:
purple juice of plums running down my chin

chewing the bitter stalks of wild fennel
harvesting bruised leaves of miner's lettuce
when the hunt for gold in the creek has failed.

One day a new house awaits our lives.
Boxes filled with indoor possessions
empty rooms booming with indoor discussions.

You find me behind the blackberry bush
slipping fruit off the tangled thicket
sick with the eating and sick with the going.

The arched stems cocoon me, as if knowing
there are times I do not want to be moved.

Altitude

after Kay Ryan

The air at this height
is fresh, like the sweet scent
of lover's breath years
before you get bored
and feel like rolling
over and pretending
sleep to take cover
from the exhalations
of his close-up
fermenting passions.

Rhapsody

I love the thunder of success
as it crumples in on itself.
I love the fracture of confidence,
where no amount of plaster
can wrap it clean and smooth again.
I love the rising dust of failure,
the inhalations of ambition
clogging every lung.

I love the rattle of a relationship
as it begins to fall apart.
The contrapuntal arguments
fighting for space on the stave,
the polyphonic misunderstandings
refusing to resolve to the root.

I love the damaged cells of nostalgia
as they infect weak muscle and bone.
I love the fossilisation of memory
as it crusts over and freezes
like time, in a dent of stone.

Frank McKenna

Frank McKenna has been dabbling in short story and poetry writing for many years. He likes a wide range of writers but favours short stories with a mix of humour and the absurd, and has been influenced by, among others, Donald Barthelme and Robert Coover.

Service

Bonny's Diner is a greasy spoon just off the motorway between London and Manchester. I sit down at the counter, two seats in from the door. The waitress is mid-forties, bleached blonde and world-weary. She lumbers up to my end of the counter and gives me a blank, bored stare, not even trying to brush the lank, loose strands of hair from her face. She has bags under her eyes, a mustard stain on her pink uniform just above her right breast and a fish-mouth fixed in a disillusioned sneer.

"Coffee. Black, no sugar. And a slice of pecan pie."

She gives me a cold, bitter look and goes off behind a green door. She comes back five minutes later and slops a mug of coffee on the counter in front of me.

"No pe*caw*n pie today." Her accent hovers somewhere between Birmingham and New York, doing justice to neither.

"Mmmm." I return her stare. "Okay, I'll have the cherry pie then."

She walks slowly down to an empty display stand at the far end of the counter, looks at it mournfully for a few seconds, comes back.

"No cherry pie today neither."

"I see. I'll try a slice of your pumpkin pie."

She looks over her left shoulder, turns her head slowly, looks over her other shoulder. "We don't have no pumpkin pie."

"I'll just have some apple pie, then."

She shrugs, gives the shelf beside the green door a cursory glance. "We don't got no more apple pie today."

"Peach and pineapple pie?"

Here she musters her most disdainful look. "WE. DON'T. NEVER. HAVE. NO. PEACH-AND-PINEAPPLE. PIE."

"Some plain old peach pie?"

"Nope. We don't have no peach pie."

"Alright. Just give me some of the blackberry pie."

"Uh-uh." She shakes her head ever-so-slightly.

"Bumbleberry pie?"

She raises one eyebrow. The corners of her mouth plunge to unfathomable depths. "I ain't never heard of no bumbleberry pie."

"Walnut pie?"

"No walnut pie here."

"Custard?"

With an exasperated snort she takes a custard pie from beneath the counter. Keeping her eyes fixed on mine, she cuts it into six perfectly equal slices. She slides the whole thing onto a cardboard cake plate, balances it expertly on one hand, and with a slow, smooth movement, pushes it into my face.

I let the bulk of it fall in my lap before wiping the rest off my face, licking little bits of the custard and the crumbled pastry, savouring its sweetness. I take a sip of my coffee. It's cold and bitter. I drink half of it down in one go.

I take out a twenty and spread it on the counter.

Her mouth straightens, the lips a thin, dark line. I'm guessing this is her smile.

I heave a deep and satisfied sigh.

"See you next week, then, Betty."

"See you, honey."

I leave.

John Flynn

John Flynn was born in Sligo but has lived in Raheny with his wife and children since 1987. John is a member of the Raheny Library Writers' Group. His writing was published in the group's collection *The Story Hatchers* in 2018.

Sheila

No weekend traffic.
A bird chirrups.
I boil the kettle,
look out my window.

Months now at home:
Am I a recluse?
Walls grey as my hair.
Later I might turn on the radio.
Silence is the gift of Covid-19.

My thoughts keep company,
memories mostly:
a country childhood,
Civil Service years
that came and went.
I'm pensioned off,
solitary.

I hear my father's voice,
my mother playing piano
in her Chanel suit …
Ah, the kettle's boiled.
Shall I dress?
A lady always does.
Clothes, my constant love.

I know this can't last,
in a few years I'll be too frail,
but for now …
For now lockdown is solitude.
I'll wear a nice suit.

A little Mozart later,
Mother's favourite.
I will water the plants,
prepare some lunch –
something festive.
It's almost Christmas after all.

The church bell in the distance,
intoning solitude:
Mass now on TV.
'There is grace in seclusion,'
Father used to say.
He wanted me to marry
but I preferred my own company.
'She's self-sufficient,' Mother said.

I buried both within two years.
Like a bereft songbird
I became mute,
the grief is with me still.
I pour my tea,
a slice of toast with butter.

My shopping is delivered,
my banking is online:
I am self-sufficient,
and wouldn't have it any other way.
Lockdown is no different,
my thoughts for company.
I've taken up crochet.
I find it restful.

Funny how noisy silence is.
Funny how crowded is solitude.
No wonder people hurry out
trying to find quiet in crowds.

Some cleaning to be done,
every day is new.
I'll make another cup of tea,
then I really will dress.
Look, it's brightening up.
I'll wave at some children from the balcony.

Everything passes,
change is constant.
The nursing home is already booked:
I will let them know when.
It will be noisy there,
but that's the price I must pay
to preserve my dignity,
and die as I was born:
self-sufficiency surrendered
on my final journey home.

Nuala Collins

Nuala Collins is a member of the Raheny Library Writers' Group. She was content to hibernate during Covid-19. She slept less and wrote more and when sleep didn't come, she wrote some more. She sketched on napkins, typed into notes, composed in her head and scribbled on her hands a myriad of ideas, inspirations, secrets and settings; all as plausible as this pandemic. Nuala took one day at a time using the best tool she knew: her creative compass. Nuala is still here. She's still writing.

Alone

He rubbed his eyes, just in case, but the lights continued to flicker even when his eyes were closed. The ribbons and tinsel and sweets and toys, the tree – both fairy-tale-like and frightening. Was this magic? Sam wondered. He couldn't remember much about his other Christmases but somehow this tree in this new home brought back images of TV ads and movies with trees that looked almost like this one. He couldn't match a movie to any particular home or family but sometimes the same movie featured more than once. He particularly liked the one where the little boy was at home alone and had to protect himself from the bad guys. He remembered some of his other families laughing at this movie and sometimes he laughed too but there were parts that were definitely not funny. Those parts always made Sam's tummy hurt.

Standing small, taking in the sights and smells of both the tree and his new home, Sam felt a familiar unease. He *hated* new homes. They always seemed nice at first but then ... He placed his chubby hands on his tummy and felt a pain that was his alone. Not a nice feeling. It wasn't the same kind of soreness as when he'd broken his ankle, the time he'd been pushed off that other boy's bike. Nor was it like when your body spills out its own blood, like when he scraped his shin on Morrison's wall and couldn't stop the bleeding. This pain was an enemy deep inside. An invisible pain that the clever doctors couldn't fix, even with all their fancy beeping machines. Now Sam knew the tears would come. The same way thunder always comes after lightening. And once the tears started to flow there was no hiding the sissy he really was.

His eyes hurt and he wondered if he closed them and gave them a little rub before opening them, she might appear. Magic but real at the same time, just like the Christmas tree. Poof! But he wasn't a magician. He was only Sissy Sam. Sometimes, if he was lucky, he was a blessing from heaven; other times he was a runt, a bastard, a waste of space. Then he remembered all at once that he was a cash cow. In the same moment he remembered one of his mothers, who wasn't really his mother, cuddling him and calling him a little lamb. This only confused Sam further, for surely everybody knew the difference between a cow and a lamb.

Sometimes adults just didn't make sense. And sometimes, Sam knew, children were more intelligent than adults, like the time Mr Barker gave out about his fizzy beers and swore he'd left twelve in the fridge. At the time Mrs Barker had insisted there were six, when both Sam and she knew quite well that Mrs Barker had in fact hid six of Mr Barker's bottles. That was one of their little secrets. But Mrs Barker wasn't all that clever, because there was still a fight. If she had really been clever, she would have hidden all twelve, and Sam struggled with just how silly Mrs Barker was then. But still, she was his favourite. Of all of them. As his warm, damp palms slid over his tender tummy, Sam missed her even more than usual. He felt his face grow wet as he slumped down at the base of the pine tree.

'Santa,' he whispered, 'if you're listening, can I please just be with Mrs Barker? I know this new house is wonderful and the tree is tall and sparkly, and they even have a dog, but I don't really want a present and I'd be happy to swap it for Mrs Barker.' But only her. Mr Barker could go to hell, even though that wasn't a nice thing to think and certainly not say.

And that was another thing. Sometimes Mrs Barker used to tell him to be quiet when Mr Barker returned home in the evenings and to stay out of his way because maybe he was tired or perhaps he had had a long day. But Sam had learned the clock and every day was the same, so when adults spoke of short or long days they weren't being clever at all. Somebody needed to teach Mrs Barker the clock. She seemed to know when the big hand reached twelve and the little hand reached seven, because then she'd busy herself with what he knew to be mumbo jumbo. He remembered when he was accused once of exactly the same thing. He'd been with another mother who wasn't his real mother then, and he was so nervous around her that his words got muddled. He remembered they were tangled in his tummy and when they came out, he imagined they were like threads of dancing spaghetti in the air. And it would have made absolutely no difference if his words were alphabet spaghetti, for they still got mixed up. Even he couldn't fix them, and so she scolded him for what she called his mumbo jumbo. Anyway, between Mrs Barker's mumbo jumbo and the banging and sometimes breaking of her pots and dishes, one thing was sure: the time was always almost seven o'clock and Mr Barker always almost home.

What Sam couldn't understand was how earlier, during the day, Mrs Barker would be gentle, kind and fun. Her soft words as clear as a shiny glass but without the sparkly bubbles. She spoilt him rotten with trips to the park and the ice cream parlour after she picked him up from school. It was Sundays that she didn't seem her usual nice Mrs Barker.

Sundays were just like a lucky bag: you never knew what you got in the Barkers' house. For one, Mr Barker rarely left the house on Sundays, and when he did you never knew for how long he'd be gone. The waiting was nearly worse than the knowing. It was almost as bad as wondering what your next mother, who wouldn't really be your mother, might be like.

Secondly, sometimes Mr Barker just shuffled around the house looking down at his shoes and mumbling. His mumbling wasn't like Mrs Barker's mumbo jumbo, but it was a jumble of words and grunts all the same, and no matter how clever you were, you still could not understand what Mr Barker was saying. And then there was dinnertime on Sundays. The only noise to be heard was the scraping of the knife or fork or spoon against Mrs Barker's pretty plates or the swallowing of dinners; and Sam could hear *everyone's* swallowing. In Sam's case his tummy also hurt but this was normal most dinner times and had absolutely nothing to do with Mrs Barker's lovely food.

In those quiet moments at Sunday dinners Sam wished the days would stay daytime forever and Mr Barker would go home someplace else at seven o'clock. Sometimes the way Mr Barker looked at Sam made him believe that Mr Barker could read minds and he would immediately stop his thoughts repeating themselves. He tried to comfort himself by remembering his pretty teacher with the funny earrings and one lesson in particular. She had enthusiastically explained how the earth moved around the sun and how impossible it would be to stop day becoming night and night becoming day. Damn it! Mr Barker didn't like Sam and both Mrs Barker and Sam knew it, but what Mr Barker didn't know was that neither Sam nor Mrs Barker liked Mr Barker. This was another one of their secrets. What Sam would never know was why Mrs Barker had married Mr Barker in the first instance. Then he remembered that nice teacher again, with her dangly moon and stars hanging from her ears in shimmers of gold that sparkled like the baubles and lights on the tree above him. That same teacher had also taught the class that sometimes opposites attract. Sam knew she was referring to many things, including people, and she'd certainly got that right with Mr and Mrs Barker. He thought of the Velcro on his shoes and how two sides were completely different but a pair nonetheless. Or when the batteries for the remote control could only work if each battery were side-by-side but placed in opposite directions. Was day and night another example? Some things just didn't make sense and Mr and Mrs Barker were one of those things, a riddle almost, only not a very fun one.

He stretched out on the carpet, his back flat on the floor, and as he did so he caught sight of his reflection in a low-hanging bauble on the branch directly above. His cheeks seemed pudgier, his nose enlarged. He delicately tipped the bauble until it swayed just like the pendulum on an old grandfather clock in one of his previous homes. The gentle force seemed to hypnotise the bauble and it swung in perfect time with the ticking of the wall clock. As the knot in his tummy eased, Sam could feel his heart beating as it too joined in the rhythm of the ticking clock and the swaying bauble. Something inside him softened.

He was back once again in the park with Mrs Barker, this time feeding the ducks. He was so happy he felt he could float like a balloon at a birthday party. Mrs Barker let him break the bread and hold the bag, and when all the ducks had had their fill she treated both of them to their favourite ice cream. Vanilla was always Mrs Barker's choice, even though she took ages to choose. Sam liked the bubble-gum flavour. It never failed to turn his lips and teeth a *shocking cobalt blue*. They were Mrs Barker's words, and Sam liked her description because it always made her giggle. And so he thought for that very reason that the bubble-gum flavour was good for Mrs Barker, even though she never took a single taste.

That was the only time he ever saw her shiny mirror. It had a great big yellow flower on it, but so small it not only fit in her handbag but could be hidden in her small hand and no one would notice. Sam secretly thought the mirror was for him, to show him his blue tongue, because never once did Mrs Barker look in the mirror herself. He also knew she didn't need to because Mrs Barker was beautiful, inside and out. Even a stranger in the park would know how beautiful Mrs Barker was, even if they'd only met her just the once.

Some fake snow fell softly just then onto Sam's face. It reminded him of the baby powder Mrs Barker used to pat onto his skin after his baths. He thought he could smell her now: a blend of talcum powder and something lemony. The scent came from the artificial branches and ornaments above him, tickling his nose. Surely this was heaven, he thought. He imagined her reflection in the baubles smiling back at him and hardly even felt the tears trickling into his ears and meandering down onto his neck. At least, not until Mrs Browne turned on the living room lights and zapped his fantasy.

This new mother gently tugged him out from under the tree, hauled him onto her lap and held him to her. She cupped her soft hands around his damp little face. She smelt nothing like Mrs Barker, but her eyes were similar somehow, and the soreness in his tummy knocked from the inside as if to be let out. She held him tighter, but not so tight it hurt. She told him to go ahead and cry, insisting he made sure to empty out all his tears. That he should use her hands as a bucket, and that she wasn't moving until both he and she knew there were no more tears left inside. Sam wasn't sure if this was even possible, for how could anyone know how many tears were inside? Maybe this was something adults just knew. So he let her hold him, feeling warm and safe, inhaling a new scent that was not sweet but comforting even so. When he realised his tears were flowing. he didn't try to stop them, and soon the pain in his tummy started to fade. It was hard to breathe at first but when he eventually caught a deep breath, the new air met the place where his pain always hid, where the doctors could never find it. Sam began to feel a little lighter inside, like a balloon.

The clock chimed and Sam knew exactly what time it was. Seven o'clock. Only this time he was at Mrs Browne's house. This new mother held him tenderly as she massaged her long fingernails over his scalp. They were sharp but soothing and Sam wondered if this might also be a type of opposites attracting.

By now he knew he was starting to doze off. Her mumbo jumbo came drifting by, accompanied by a soft melody he liked. One thing was clear now, no matter how tired Sam felt: for all Mrs Browne's whispering words that evening, she kept repeating the same three in the same order. Sam thought it may have been a favourite story of hers but if it was, he had never heard of The Little Fostered Lamb.

He felt happy and safe, for now at least. He was getting better at recognising these moments, he knew, and allowing himself to feel their magic. Chances were he would move home again, but for now, for right now, Sam wasn't going to think about that. This was one of the special moments and he would treasure it for as long as he could.

Sleep came easily, and brought with it a new lightness in his tummy. He felt himself floating away, as if he were his very own balloon.

Sinéad MacDevitt

Sinéad MacDevitt contributes to the Ballyfermot Library Writers' Group. Her work has been published in *Boyne Berries, Extended Wings, Revival Literary Journal, The Reform Jewish Quarterly, The Flying Superhero Clothes Horse* and *Mustang Bally*. She was shortlisted for the Swords Heritage Festival short story competition and highly commended in the Jonathan Swift prose competition. Her poems were commended for the Francis Ledwidge, LMFM and Rush Poetry competitions. In 2013, she was awarded second prize for the Desmond O'Grady competition.

From the Qafe e Thelle (Deep Pass)
Albania 2019

Aga!
Ardian's call rolls into waves

that fade above the dip of the Deep Pass.
Aga!

No sign but the yap and the snap
from a quiver of black fur in a patch of green.

The creature may be a sheepdog
and we may be walking Byron's footsteps

but this is the dog's territory
while the shepherd is away.

No ring of a bell
round the neck of a goat.

No sound of a clop or a trot
or a whoop from a muleteer.

So we turn towards the Llogara Pass:
the peak and pines become an imprint

and the crunch of stones beneath
tracks my own story.

Memories of Seán O'Carroll Street, Ardee

On reflection of an incident on 30th November 1920

The whisper from the hearth,
the jig from the transistor
that filters beyond apple trees,
censor the scenes of the Twenties.

Footsteps through Castle Street
towards the riverside walk
on a Sunday afternoon,
deaden a murmur: a march.

Memories of the station's
phantom whistle from Dromin,
the clock of the street,
mutes a soldier's patrol.

A row of redbrick homes
where my aunt used to live,
now on black and white prints,
evoke the boom of the gun.

Through the grassy path,
once flowered by Uncle Bill,
his orchard is like a sketch:
a row of limbs for the chop.

On my return to the street
where bruised apples drop,
a sculpture remains:
the captain who was shot.

My eyes travel faster
than the post towards
the tower, beyond the pale
to the Mull of Kintyre.

The Cliff of Fingal

Before bricks begin to rise, there'll be time
    to journey as far as Meath's traffic to the Naul

        and cycle past fields of reeds that climb the sky
           and hear the cows lowing and the shepherds' sign.

Once again I will travel through the road
    or lane that's still divided by the grass

        and wonder if this will lead to a turn or cul-de-sac
           or village or townland or a farmer's land.

And I will record the sounds before the dawn,
    before I forget the difference between trill and phone

        and flying trails of feather and of steel and watch
           branches that swirl the shades of Fingal's scene.

And I will get the chance to trace the steps,
    to where the White Castle was once built

        and recreate the stairs that Cadell climbed
           and try to view the races in Bellewstown.

Before the dusk closes in again
    long after Cromwell ruined Black Castle in 1649,

I will take time to capture the ivied walls
and fractured stairwell that leads to the unknown.

Before the news at nine, I'll get a chance
to celebrate the dampness of the soil

that fills the air during the walk to Hynestown's hill,
remembered by a Dubliner in a village school.

And I will get to photograph the street
and capture Reilly's Daybreak and the Big Tree,

the cottages, thatched roofs and Killian's bar
before the city's double decker bus appears.

Mary O'Callaghan

Mary O'Callaghan lives in Raheny with her family, and has been a member of Raheny Library Writers' Group for a few years. She has a keen interest in local history, and she teaches English language classes. She has written various books, including *Three Weeks in the Gaeltacht: A memoir* and *Growing Up Word by Word: A memoir about reading and writing as a child*.

My Grandad

My Cork grandad used to visit us in Dublin every couple of months when we were growing up. When I knew him he was a widower in his early seventies. He always wore a neat suit, perhaps a dark grey one. If he was outdoors, he tended to wear a trilby hat. His parents had been a tailor and a dressmaker, and he was always smartly turned out. He was quiet-spoken and had a gentlemanly manner.

We had our breakfast in the dining room, rather than the kitchen, when my grandfather visited. The marmalade, usually in its shop jar, would, for the occasion, be put in the colourful ceramic marmalade pot. My grandad would smile and chat and give a couple of very big yawns with outstretched arms. Then he would eat his boiled egg and slices of toast, and have a cup of tea. His toast was cut into triangles, whereas the rest of us ate rectangles.

He would also be handed the newspaper, the *Irish Times*. He was given the privilege of being the first to read it. When breakfast finished up, he would open the newspaper, stretching it fully open, and, for a few minutes, I would only be able to see the spread-out newspaper and the backs of my grandad's pale hands.

He liked walks. He walked in nearby St. Anne's Park and along the Bull Wall down at the seafront. He seemed to really like the sea. I was surprised when he said that in Cork he lived quite a long way from the sea. I had assumed that everyone lived near the sea. When we visited him in Cork, we might go for a long walk in the countryside.

My grandad liked to walk with my family in Dublin, but also on his own. I was surprised, when he went for walks on his own, that someone could be happy in their own company.

In the afternoons he would sit by the fire in the sitting-room in our house. There he would smoke cigarettes with a black filter. He would finish reading the paper and do the crossword. He was not pushed about television, and in the evenings we would read our books together, quietly by the fire.

He was very fond of us, his grandchildren. When he saw us his face lit up. He always seemed interested in what we had to say. A retired teacher and school principal, he was good with children. Sometimes I felt a little shy with him, if I hadn't seen him in a while, but he knew how to put me at my ease. He would ask me simple spellings, and then look very impressed when I got them right. After that I would chat away to him confidently.

My grandad also knew how to entertain us. He told me about a leprechaun and his pot of gold at the end of the rainbow. He sang us songs and asked us riddles, e.g., "What goes up and down at the same time?" (A hill). One time he brought a conch shell as a present, and got us to put it to our ears, so that we could 'hear' the sea.

Occasionally he would mention his past, a nice car he'd once had, or something about the school in which he had taught. He sometimes said things that made me think. For instance, one day someone made a remark about not wanting grey hair, and he said, "And what's wrong with grey? It's a nice colour."

My grandad told us that when he was in Cork he went out for his dinner each day to a hotel, and that this cost three pounds. I was surprised someone would go to a hotel each day, but I suppose, looking back, an elderly widower in the 1970s would not have known how to cook.

I was keen on sewing, knitting and crochet. My grandad would ask me about my work. At one stage, he asked about a small, crocheted quilt that I was making. How was I deciding which colours to use? What different designs was I choosing for its squares? How was I going to arrange the squares? I suppose the teacher in him was getting me to think about what

I was doing, to try to figure out the best way of doing things. Also, he had a genuine liking for well-designed objects. His house contained several antiques which he had bought over the years, such as pairs of attractive old jugs on his sitting room mantelpiece.

I was surprised, but pleased, that he was interested in my craft work. It made me look at my crochet, and so on, in a new light. Maybe it was more serious, more significant, than I had realised. Maybe I should think carefully about what I was doing.

My grandad gave me various presents. For instance, he gave me a Celtic "Tara" brooch and a little gold cross with a diamond in the middle. I think the cross was for my First Communion. I was pleased to be given 'grown-up' presents.

He gave me books too, including a book of Grimm's fairytales, a book about courageous people, and one about wild animals. I really liked them. The book about courageous people helped spark my life-long interest in history. My grandad usually wrote an inscription when he gave a present of a book. Sometimes I was asked by a parent to write a thank you letter to him for a present. I would spend a good while composing those letters. I wanted to send my grandad more than a thank you; I wanted to tell him my news.

I was sad when my grandad got sick, from cancer, and started using a walking stick. Occasionally now, when he came to visit, I went on little errands to the shop for him. I didn't realise how sick he was. After a few months he went into hospital, and there was mention of him being very sick. Still, I was shocked when he died, a few days after I turned ten. I remember the moment that I was told very clearly, as I headed home from school one afternoon in June.

There was a guard of honour outside the church for the funeral, made up of boys from the school in which my grandad had been principal. After the mass, a couple of adults that I didn't know came over to me, introduced themselves, and said how sorry they were that my grandfather had died. I felt a bit shaken when I saw an adult relation weeping.

Then we, the family, got into the funeral cars, and, as the funeral cortege slowly moved along through the town, people on the sides of the road stood and watched sadly, and doffed their hats in respect. We went back to my grandad's house for sandwiches after the funeral. It was strange being there without him. I spotted his walking stick in the hallway.

I felt a special connection to my grandad. I think we understood each other. It was hard losing him, and I miss him still. I have my memories, so that's something. And every so often there's still a point of connection. Years back, I read a lovely piece online that a former pupil wrote about him. I would occasionally look at old photos; at one stage, I realised he was the only person I knew who had the same 'button' nose as me. When I started going to antique fairs, I was glad to hear that he used to go to them too. I also learnt that the Gaeltacht I went to as a youngster was the one he had gone to as well.

In his will, he left me his watch, an elegant ebony conductor's baton he used as a pointer when teaching, a silver bonbon dish and a silver napkin ring, as well as some money. The watch was a surprising thing to leave a young girl. It was an item that he would have used every day, and I was pleased that he wanted me to have it. It's the teaching baton, though, that has an extra significance for me now as an adult. Perhaps he guessed that I would one day be a teacher like him.

Frances Gaynor

Frances Gaynor is from Dublin and writes poetry and fiction. She gets wonderful support from her membership of the Donaghmede Library Writers' Group and is currently working on her first novel.

Massage

"Just breathe in ..."
Your supple fingers quickly
Find my knots, swim
Straight to the rocks in the sea of my skin.
"Breathe out ..."

Unmasked, downward facing,
My slack mouth drools as you
Smooth the lumpen strains
In the muscles of my back.
"And again, deep breath in ..."

I am not allowed lie
Beached on the plinth:
I must engage for you
To achieve your purpose
Of giving release.

"I want to know how you breathe."
You sound concerned.
I work hard to develop a rhythm,
Catch myself holding
My breath, concentrating.

Your hand is like silk
Slipping over my limbs,
And when you take my hand
The forbidden gesture makes me wince,
Then makes me exhale.

Your face dips at the cash desk
When you tell me I need to
Practice breathing. You have caught
Me out in the bad habit
Of holding my breath.

I promise to practice, and
Thank you for the validation.

Return

Her distant past closes in.

As if on an elastic band,
She pulled away
From her point of origin,
Stretched herself
Along new pathways
Following her nose
And dreams,
Rolled with the punches;
At the farthest point,
Cried, recognising no home.

In the first chamber now
Of the torture of old age –
The pain, the organ removal,
The staving off of the worst of it
With pills and sweet treats –
She lies in her made bed
Listening carefully; sits
In her customised chair, turning
From the magazine
To face who is coming.

She thinks they are all coming:
The man in the red home-knit
Pullover and flat cap is perched
On her bed when she wakens

Mid-morning. She gapes.
He rises, pleasant, and disappears.
She feels this is portentous:
It brings tears to her eyes
But the only words she finds
Or is willing to share is that

There is a presence about her home
Of late. She says she doesn't feel
Dread or a sense of danger.
Although she is crying,
She feels safe, she says.
Her voice shrinks and flies back
Into her mouth like a startled bird
As she muses, "It's probably Mammy."
Her face is unwiped.
Who is coming home to whom?

She seems to feel ghosts all around her,
But will only give half-hints about
Their presence, is guarded in telling
Me – a resident of elsewhere –
What is going on. The air grows thick
Between us, mother and daughter.

She cries like a child
Who knows she is tired
But does not want to go to bed yet.

Dún Aonghasa

Ocean spring green:
Pastel impressions belie
Gunmetal grey depths.

Air soft-white, soft
Breath of light inhaled
From the height that grounds.

Tourists at liberty now
To come and take leave,
Unhindered but watched

By scions and ghosts
Of the old clans.
Spanish infants like

Brightly coloured lambs
On the mossy lawn.
Beneath the fronded cloak

Of Dún Aonghasa,
Limestone foundations bare
Their bruised knuckles.

Katarina Timulakova

Katka joined the Raheny Library Writers' Group few years ago. She was born in Czechoslovakia behind the Iron Curtain. As a teenager she has witnessed the Velvet Revolution, cultural changes and the split of the country. She studied and worked in Slovakia before moving to Dublin with her family. When she wants to remember a particular moment or a feeling, she paints it on canvas or writes it in a story.

Three Peeks Behind the Iron Curtain

1: A kid from the block

Our family lived on the fifth floor of an eight-floor concrete building. The apartment had three bedrooms, one where I lived with my parents, and one each for my older sisters. The balcony faced high mountains. The light during the day coloured them different hues: blue in the morning, gold in the afternoon, and softening to pinks and purples by evening.

Far below the balcony was a winding river. In winter it became a wide, long skating rink. Sometimes the water froze so suddenly that sleeping swans got stuck and people used axes to break them out of the ice.

Across the river was a military base where you could see the conscripted young men exercising all day long. They could see you too. You would not wear a bikini to sunbathe unless you liked wolf-whistles. Teenage soldiers are friendly in person, though, as we discovered during Open Days. We used their obstacle trail and climbed into stationary tanks.

Next to the apartment block on the left side was another apartment block, of the same height and structure – its twin. The laced windows of the mirror image of our flat made me paranoid. I worried that someone was watching me with their binoculars. Sometimes I took out *our* binoculars to check I wasn't being watched. I never saw anything suspicious, but I kept checking.

Next to the twin building were garages along one edge of a car park. Not every family had a car, but more families got one over the years. Cars were meant to last a lifetime. Our car was about twenty years old, a Skoda 100. My mom learnt how to drive when she was young, but after her first drive she flipped the car over and never tried again. It became dad's car after that.

On the right side of the block was the green, a children's playground, and a small courtyard with chickens that belonged to an old man. There were plenty of opportunities for we children to invent games. We used see-saws, the sandpit, climbing racks and a slide to make games of chasing interesting. Chasing could go on for hours. The little space on the building wall was a touch-down for hide-and-seek. The hiding places during the daylight were out of sight: behind corners and big bushes, or hiding between small children and their parents in the playground. When darkness fell, the high, uncut grass mixed with weeds provided the perfect hiding place.

In front of our apartment block was a carpet-beating rack. Everyone would hang from the rack and the blindfolded kid on the ground had to reach for someone and guess who they were. Other children called out to confuse the catcher. We shrieked with joy, but the mothers of small children from the balconies on the lowest floors would get angry. They feebly tried to shoo us away, as if we were annoying flies keeping their children awake.

2: Olympic Games

As a child in the 1980s, the majority of my summer holidays were spent outdoors and unsupervised. In our eight-floor apartment block there were 32 families and 54 children. Kids older than two were minded by other children, as the adults had to work. Any adult who did not work ended up in jail. And then they were made to work there.

In my extended friend group of about 20 kids from our block, the youngest child was just over two years old and the oldest 14. One year we organised an Olympic Games. It was 1988, the year when the real

Games were held in Seoul. We gathered on the grass meadow. Around 20 countries were represented. I chose Japan, as I felt it was a developed country. You would hate to be left with a country like Bulgaria or Ukraine, as they weren't considered cool. We did high jumping, long jumping and running. Two kids held a bar at an estimated height that would be slightly increased, and the rest of the children attempted to leap over. When I jumped over the bar, I landed on the hard grassy ground, which was very painful. But I wouldn't cry.

The best jumper received an award of a thistle, which stuck well to clothes – so well, in fact, that no mother was impressed trying to take it off later. Sergey Bubka, the Russian jumper, won a gold medal in the pole vault at Seoul, so we named our highest jumper after him.

3: The music concert and the secret police

Two years before Mikhail Gorbachev used the term *Perestroika* for the first time, I went to my first music concert. My parents were still worried about being caught tuning in to the *Hlas Ameriky* (Voice of America) radio station. They were still hiding religious books behind the secular ones on shelves, and worried that their salaries would be affected should someone inform that I'd had my First Holy Communion (secretly, in a different town).

That was the year my mom showed me a manager from her work, who was a secret agent. She told me that he meddled with her salary following my sister's Confirmation in our local church. That explained the secrecy around my sacrament.

Our town only had fifteen thousand or so inhabitants, which was why music bands came rarely. So news about a popular heavy metal band's arrival got me excited. Tublatanka took their name from Tublat, an ape who hates Tarzan. I was ten at the time, and with my two younger friends walked up to be near the outdoor venue where the band were playing. The venue was surrounded by forest, and two songs in we met boys from our estate and got smuggled in through the hole in the fence.

I was more smitten by the long-haired fans in denim than I was with the musicians. We imitated their hair-shaking with our short 'helmet' haircuts. My favourite song was *We'll Try To Get Out Through the Universe*, and I danced and sang my heart out.

By then it was getting dark and we needed to go home. With no tickets to show on the way out, we returned to the hole in the fence. At that point a police officer and an agent with the Secret Police (you know which one – just my luck) caught us. The agent asked for my name. He checked if I was a daughter of [my mother]. I confirmed that I was, and he let us all go.

I cried all the way home with the weight of putting my mother's job in jeopardy, but afterwards I never heard her saying anything about the concert.

In 2017 I watched Tublatanka in concert in Dublin. They were on tour to celebrate their 33rd anniversary tour – which meant my very first concert was during their very first tour.

Terri Jade Donovan

Terri Jade Donovan is a disabled and hard of hearing actor and writer currently based in Dublin. Her writing specialises in playwriting and poetry.

The Magpie (extract)

The mist clung to the green.
A silver thread of threat
Spooling itself around
The bulging shrubs and dropping violets
In the sleeping, cinched square.
The railings, draped low round the vast grounds,
Let not even the whisper of a slim shadow
Cross their boundary
Into the park.
The hours of welcome long faded; now
Only the mist,
This lingering mist,
Folds itself across a desert of itching calm.

Hush now,
Sink deeper into the surrounding darkness
And wait,
For the clock, high up on the pepper-church loft
Notches her hands on,
Tugging time towards

The hour that sits
On the tooth of the ghoul,
Or on the tip of the nib-like claw
Of the muttering beast,
Or on the eyelash of a hag
That jilts her green chin out
From under your childhood bed.
Here, now, the creatures that sweep past your
Young sleeping form
Gather in your mind
At the lonely hour
Where magic hangs
By a spider's thread.

Look, she approaches.

A magpie, fattened by midnight's old feathers
And moon-cut chest
Flutters down into the pool of descending mist.
Resting her claws finally upon the soaked earth,
She throws her head from side to side,
Tail hilted up. The eyes flash,
Dark orbs questing,
Hunting for a slithering feast.

But now there are other eyes,
Watching her switch and swagger:
Eyes of violent amber that
Widen from the edge of the clearing.

Body drawn low, ears pricked, with paws
Clenched, his slim coat and snout has nestled itself
Amongst this darkness we cling to,
And like us, he waits,
impatient for the witching hour to strike –

Snap! Her head springs up from its pickings
To pour her eyes into the heady mass of night,
Which, 'til now, had been as a choked silence
in a swelling storm –
Eyes still darting, throwing her wings open,
And as she jerks her head back
His paws retract, trembling –

Enda Halpin

Enda Halpin is originally from Collon, Co. Louth, and has been living in Dublin since the early 70's. Married to Anne for 45 years, they are proud parents of Conor, Aoife and Neasa, and doting grandparents to five grandchildren. A retired HSE Manager, Enda is a member of the Donaghmede Library Writers' Group.

Missing

Dear David,

I painted your room this week, a sort of light grey. Elephant's Breath, it's called. Strange name. But it gave me something to do.

Apart from that, your room is the same as it always was. I'm still hoping. So I keep it ready. You should never give up hope, when you do there's nothing left. You become a memory, remembered only on birthdays and anniversaries. Your father says that's what you are now, but not to me. I read about that girl in Austria, missing for what, eight years? And she came back. Her mother said she'd known in her heart she was still alive. So you see. You will always be alive to me.

The police were good, in the beginning. That first day.

"Look missus, he's probably just gone for a day or two, to make you suffer, make you worry. Kids are like that, they can be cruel, thoughtless, don't think. Maybe you had a row, I'll bet you did, and he's taking it too hard. A sensitive chap, is he? Thinks about things, I'll bet. Just looking at his photograph here I'd say he is. And you can't say a word to kids today or you're accused of all sorts. Is there a friend or relative he might be staying with? Could he be hiding in one of his friend's houses without their parents knowing?"

I told them no, of course not. You weren't that type of child. You wouldn't do that to us, your family, you would never make us worry like that. You're not like that.

"Most missing kids come back safely in a day or two, a week at the most. They miss their home comforts, and boys miss their mother. Ninety-nine percent of them return. The odds are in your favour."

But what about the one per cent, I asked. He might be one of those.

"Let's just wait and see," he said. They did regard you as high risk though, from the beginning, they told me that.

I'll never forget phoning your friends that first evening. "Have you seen David? Do you know where he might be?" Then going to the police station that evening, being told about the ninety-nine percent, being told you have to be missing for 24 hours before the police start looking. Screaming at them, your father dragging me out of the station, and me cursing them for their statistics. Then driving around the town all night as the panic set in, and I just knew something was wrong, as wrong as wrong can be. Then your picture on television, on the papers, the continuous discussions with the police, the investigation into the family, our friends, your life, our lives, your friends. That was gut-wrenchingly hard.

But after a year there were no new leads, no sightings, no hope of a breakthrough. I bombarded the police with phone calls and visits. They were apologetic, they were sorry for me, but I could tell I was an embarrassment, a nuisance. "We have other cases, other missing people, other things to do." They didn't say that, but that's what they meant. Working on the ninety-nine percent.

I joined a missing persons' support group. It helps that there are people like me there, with family who have left, or gone missing, some longer than you. We support one other on Facebook, YouTube, Instagram. Inviting people to get in touch if they think they have information. To keep you in the public eye. To not let people forget. We get information from time to time, pass it on, most of it no use. But you have to check it out. And the cruellest thing: people who pretend to know. Phone calls, sometimes late at night: "Hello, I am your missing son, I'm coming home tomorrow. Did you miss me? Did you think I was dead?" Who does things like that? What sort of people are they?

But the group helps. For anniversaries and birthdays we print posters, putting them up in public places, shop windows, supermarkets. Handing them out on the street to as many people as we can.

"Did you see this child? Please look very carefully. Do you know him? Are you sure you don't? Please, please look again. Take your time. Are you absolutely sure you have never seen him?"

Some people in the group accept their loved one is never coming back, but they still want to know what happened. Closure, it's called. There could be a service, a grave, somewhere to visit, a place where you could talk. It would help.

There is someone out there, somewhere, who knows something, who could tell me where you are, and what happened. Even if they could send an anonymous message to the police, or the support group, just to let us know, to tell us where to find you.

One woman in the group, her daughter has been missing for 22 years, she still hopes. Rings the police, calls in to them. She's very strong, she inspires us all. She says she has accepted her daughter is never coming back but she never stops hoping. Working with the rest of us. Supporting us, encouraging us. Some people have accepted the worst, given up hope. But they still attend. They say they get strength from the group. That's good, isn't it? We help each other.

Your father and I split up six years ago. We blamed each other. He couldn't take it anymore, he said. My endless hoping, my obsession, my refusal to accept that you are gone and never coming back. Keeping everything the same as the day you disappeared, like a shrine, he said, buying birthday and Christmas presents. Writing to you. You know I have written to you every few months since you left? Just little letters. Keeping you up to date. Letting you know what we're doing, how we are. It helps me.

"You'll have to accept he's gone and he's not coming back. As much for your own good as anything," your father said.

He said I thought he didn't grieve as much as me. How could he think that? How can you measure grief, especially someone else's? He said it makes no sense, doing all those things. Well, it makes sense to me.

I go for long walks most days. Helps clear the head. I look at the faces of young men, about 20 or 21, your age now, who have your colouring, and look like what I think you would look like now. I stare, and sometimes I follow them.

I'm good at this, very discreet. They don't realise when I'm following them, just to get a glimpse.

Does that sound strange? I suppose it does, but I'll never stop looking for you, my beautiful boy. It helps me. No one knows that only you. I haven't told anyone in the support group. What would they think of me? That's our secret.

David, you are the first thing I think about in the morning, and the last thing I think about as I go to sleep at night. You are all I think about.

Not knowing is the worst.

The police told me that they can declare you officially dead after seven years if there's sufficient grounds for doing so. But you're not, are you? How can you be? They tell me that your status is missing, presumed dead. *I* don't presume you're dead. Sometimes when I'm low, you're missing; but mostly I try to think you're just away, that you'll walk back into my life one day. I have to think like that. For my sanity.

What happened to you, David? Where did you go? Where are you? Who knows? Sometimes I sit in your room for hours, or lie on your bed. I think about your short life and the things you loved doing. I think about the last time I saw you, that morning as you left for school, never arrived, and never came home. When you said, "I love you, Mam."

I can still hear your voice. Did I say I loved you back? Did I say I loved you more? I hope I did. Remember our little ritual?

I blame myself for what happened. I should have been more on my guard, more alert to the dangers out there, to the predators. I should have been repeating it every day. Warning you never to talk to strangers, or get into a stranger's car.

Did I do that enough? Because children go missing every day. I torture myself by thinking I didn't, that I'm somehow to blame.

They advised us to go for counselling, said it would help to talk to someone outside the family. Gave us a list of names to choose from, said it was up to us. And we did go. But I found it too painful. Sometimes after a session I felt guiltier than before. The counsellor said that's just part of the process, part of working through it, part of *accepting*. I couldn't focus on the word accepting, or that we should eventually look for *closure*. There will never be closure until I know for certain. So I stopped going.

Everything belonging to you is still here in your room. Your clothes. I bury my face in your t-shirts, inhale your smell. Long gone I know, but alive to me. Your school books, school work, football boots and gear, books, computer, CDs, DVDs, posters, the superhero figures on the window sill, the Lego castle you built when you were seven and were so proud of. The stories you made up about Oscar the Rabbit. I still read them. They are part of you, the most precious part: those stories show me the person you would have become if you were still here. When I buy your birthday and Christmas presents I have to guess what you would be interested in now, after ten long years. But I know. A mother always knows. Such a cliché, but true.

I relive your short life in those moments in your room. That's when I feel you are still here with me. I feel you're close. I call your name and sometimes I imagine I hear you running up the stairs. And then the quiet, the deathly silence. The nothing. And then I think my heart will just explode in a volcano of sorrow.

You are now gone longer than the time you were with me. There are things I can't bring myself to think about, things the police said I may have to accept some time. I know what those things are, but I can't think about them. I won't.

The last time I called to the police was about six months ago. I asked for the Superintendent in charge of your case. The sergeant on the front desk told me he wasn't there.

"Can I speak to anyone else? Who *is* in charge of my case, there must still be someone?" Then he became a bit more sympathetic.

"Look, your case is still open, we review any information that comes to us. We haven't forgotten, we still put out feelers, follow up enquiries. There's talk of referring your son's case to the Cold Case Unit."

I cling on to any glimmer of hope there is.

Jane has got a good job now, working in advertising. She missed you like crazy, her little brother. She was like a protector for you, your guardian. Always stood up for you at school, on the road with the other kids. I could hear her crying nearly every night that first year. She couldn't understand, she was too young. Only a year older than you. I couldn't help her, couldn't relieve her pain. I tried, but not hard enough. My own pain was too much.

And that was wrong. She deserved more. I should have loved her better then. Tried to ease her pain. I let her down, she was only a child herself. I failed her too.

I was missing to her as well as you. She lost her mother as well as her brother that day. Nothing can make up for that.

But she did well at college. She wanted to try to forget you, without forgetting you, if you know what I mean. To live with it somehow. Because she would never forget you.

She told me to my face that I lost interest in life because of you going missing. I think she's right. Deep down I've always known that.

But she's doing well now, has a nice boyfriend, Sean's his name. They seem happy. He's good for her. They're saving for a house. They'll probably get married at some stage. Young people aren't in a hurry these days, they take their time. They're living together, but that's alright, everyone does that now. Children now attend their parents' weddings. What a change from my day.

She calls round when she can. She doesn't stay over, she hasn't stayed overnight for years. She doesn't feel this is her home. My grieving for you has driven her away.

She visited yesterday with Sean. It's important for both of us. Trying to be normal. She will never talk to me about you, maybe she can't. She thinks I'm obsessive. And she's right, but to give up is to let you go and I can't do that.

I overheard her saying to Sean that she can't stay in this house any longer than an hour or so. Maybe that will change at some stage. I hope so. She told Sean I look ten years older than my age, that I don't look after myself anymore.

But here's some news. The Superintendent rang me yesterday. He wants to discuss your case. We see him tomorrow afternoon, your father and I. It brought back everything again. Another sleepless night. But that's okay. Maybe there's something new, some fresh evidence, or someone saw something. An informant, maybe? It's something to cling to. A glimmer of hope. Let's wait and see. That's all I can do.

Love you forever,

Mam

Mary Oyerdiran

Mary Oyerdiran is a radio presenter for the International Writers Network dedicated to promoting new writers. She has contributed to the yearly anthologies of Ink Splinters (for the Ballymun Library Writers' Group), and to *Candlestick* magazine. Her greatest achievement was the publication of her poetry in the *Faith, Hope & Love* anthology in 2020.

Great October

October entrusted us with Dearest Mother.
Ageless, brilliant and bright,
Her anger erupting like dynamite
And generous pounds tied in hankies.

October gave birth to two fair sons,
Strong males like chalk and cheese,
Charming princes with cheeky grins
Who grew in wisdom, escaping sins.

October, and we bring our yearly offering,
Lavishing a feast fit for an emperor,
Licensed for fun and frolicking
As Grandma and grandsons embraced.

October's hands stretched out
In fury, a canopy of darkness
Snatching our beloved teenage son,
Shattering our hearts in sadness.

October, an angry tornado roared
And whisked away our frail, infirm Mother.
No consolation but hot, bitter tears,
Our days spent shivering in the deepest fears.

October became a month to dread,
Strangled our jubilations for dead.
Ashes piled our hair, our faces torn:
Daily we sat in sackcloth so worn.

October's sun rose, angels smiling:
Has God sent us mercy, His grace?
All hearts bubbled in His face
When our daughter bore her son.

October ushered in its blessings,
Joyful rays melting all our sorrow.
Oceans of love flooding our lean souls,
Our feet skipping like deer on hind.

October! Our month, great October!
Now a sacred month to remember.
A rare bright diamond to treasure,
Our valley now filled with pleasure.

Paddy Murray

Paddy Murray was born in Dublin 72 years ago. He lived in Gardiner Place until moving to Coolock. He joined P&T as a Technician at 16, staying until retirement. He spent many childhood summers in a thatched house down a long lane. Images of town and country stayed for his children's bedtime stories. He joined Raheny Library Writers' Group in 2016, and is still Zooming along these days.

Three Letters to an Armistice

1 Pain

Old Brook Farm,
Boxgrove,
West Sussex.

For the Attention of Captain Edward Tomlinson,
Royal Sussex Regiment

Dear Sir,

It is morning again and whether I slept any of the night I can't tell. I sit here reading the telegram over and over although I know it by heart. I'm writing to you not knowing if you are alive or dead, I couldn't bring myself to ask if there were any left who knew the fate of my Jack. My Jack! My only son, my life, my future.

Now I can barely keep going from one day to the next, indeed I hardly know which day is which. I only milk the cows because the bellowing of the poor beasts rouses me from my stupor. My crops would have rotted in the fields were they not saved thanks to the kindness of friends and good neighbours. It is my wife and the womenfolk who manage to keep going, they seem to have a well of strength despite their own heartbreak. They speak in whispers around me as if at a deathbed.

In his letters Jack spoke of how you looked after the men in your company. Though he spoke little of the war, talking more about the farm and our crops and stock, I gathered that you managed to keep most of your lads safe over the years. Reading between the lines I gleaned how you went to great lengths preparing your company for action. Jack joked about the good fortune of being part of a gang of country yokels who knew how best to use the lie of the land to their advantage.

I keep tormenting myself in wondering what went wrong that night, what evil thing reached down and took my Jack. Or maybe it was what reached up? Although we hear much of the gods of war, surely what we are seeing is the Devil's work. I'm not blaming you, how could I? Who can I blame? Those who govern us and led us into this terrible war, or we, who foolishly followed? What madness came over us, especially when life was getting a bit better for ordinary folk like us farmers or the workers in the factories? Did we expect to be smitten for the sin of enjoying a little comfort?

If, like Jack, you too were lost that night, I pray that you and he and the rest of your troop have found a paradise in which to rest after your eternity in that muddy Hell. If through the grace of God you still live, please believe that you do not need to reply to this letter. I can't bear to think of what Jack went through in his last moments, so how could I wish to hear the awful truth? I want to remember him as he went away, tall and proud. I am lucky to have a father's memory when you must have the terrible memories of the last moments of many sons. Half-dead as we who have passed through this terrible epoch will always remain, I can only pray for those who have gone, not just from these islands but from the whole world over. The cattle have been calling to me this past while and at least I can relieve their suffering. Adieu. Wherever you are on Earth or in Heaven, pray for me!

Yours faithfully,

John Atkins.

2 Unposted

Craiglockhart Hospital,
Edinburgh,
7th November 1918.

Dear Sir,

I have had your letter all these months in the hospital but only now could I read it and reply to you. At first my wounds left me unable to move, but as they healed the darkness set in. You wrote about the death of your boy Jack and the years he had been in my company and his regard for me. Yes, I had managed to keep most of my command safe, until that night.

We were in No Man's Land checking the wire. Jack was one of the half-dozen of us out that night and we were almost finished when I was the one who stumbled. The shell-hole was full of water and the splash alerted the Bosch. The flares lit us up for the machine guns and, worst of all, the mortars.

I can still hear their screams and the calls for me to do something to save them. I couldn't even save myself. Lord Jesus on your Cross, did you see those lads of mine crucified on the wire? Did you take them to the Heavenly Valhalla they had earned in a Hell daily endured? Why was I the one to be resurrected when it was my mistake that doomed us? The screams died as they died and should I not have died too? No, the light and the mist awoke me and I dragged myself back to our lines. To the Field Dressing Station, the Base Hospital, and then back to England. Eventually I ended up in Scotland.

Am I writing to you to ask your understanding and forgiveness for my failure to save your son or am I only speaking to myself? Who do I tell of the demons within me? My father, who was one of those urging the nation and his sons to war against the beastly Hun, now can't even talk of the war when we meet. I think he knows that this war didn't end wars, it has opened wounds that won't heal and will be picked at again and again until the Apocalypse. There is news that the first of those Horsemen are raging through the world like some macabre conquistador.

And my Elisa, I made it back to her as I promised; and she had waited. She sits with me through the long hours and speaks of the wonderful times we shared. Elisa, as deep as she is beautiful, has a sadness in her eyes when she looks into my face. Does she see there the ghosts that haunt me, the faces without limbs, without eyes, with not mouths but bottomless howling pits? How can we speak of a future when our world has been uprooted and all the young shoots cut down?

How can I ask her to share my nights? Like some accursed beast I can live by day but when night falls the darkness is split by searing light and screams. The screaming of shells, the screams of the dying. I can't even scream but instead curl up like a beaten cur and whimper until the return of the light. Her beauty and intellect would drown just as my manhood did in that shell-hole. Could we beget children to be fed to the ravening beast we had created?

As I write this there is the hope that this terrible war will end before the week is out. Sweet Jesus let it stop!

3 Elisa's Song

Dearest Eddie,

I've been beside you since you came home, nursing you in all the different wards and hospitals you've been through. That dreadful night when your troop and your hope had all died – you called to me. Like some little bird I flew to you and with fluttering wings I parted the morning mists to bring the life of the sun onto your face. My hand was in yours then as you dragged your broken body across that blasted ground. I left you to the care of your comrades until they brought you home to me.

I know your demons and ghosts, meeting them even before you woke to their presence. You can hear the screams of your dying comrades while I can hear the cries of the children that will never know them or will never be. Still, still your fears in my arms: they are strong, stronger than Sheffield steel and can sooth tender babies and broken men.

My uniform has a Red Cross. God and Science working to heal even in the midst of battle. Soon I will have a voice in how we are governed, perhaps men and women together can forge a better world. You fear that I would not have the heart to bear children into a foolish and dangerous world. Women have always feared childbirth, desired and feared it as men do battle. It is a combat of two lives, a brutal bloody thing in which one or both may perish.

In the horrors of your nights I've been with you, waiting to bring the light to you again. I pray that your wounds or our fears won't deny us children. I know you will regain the strength to safeguard us while I nurse them as they grow into strong children with a sun-bright future filled with joyous laughter. We have learned from our pain so that instead of fearing for them, we can be guides to their own horizons, whether these be bright with promise or aflame with doubt.

> I touched you in your mother's arms the first time I met you.
> One Sunday in our village church on that old oaken pew.
> You pulled my hair and made me cry.
> "Bold boy!" your mother scolded and bade you sooth my tears.
> I knew your love as I do now, you kissed away my fears.
>
> Through the summer of our childhood we learned our secret ways.
> Our bodies and our minds were one those happy shining days.
> Not knowing that our sun would set and never rise again.
> In silent woods one chilly night I held you close to me
> To magic airs we sealed our love beneath the fairy tree.
>
> School days meant we had to part but our stars were just as clear.
> Shining on words that lit up worlds where shadows disappear.
> You wrote me love, I gave you verse to keep us ever near.
> Until we would return unto a time of me and you.
> A world for us to make, a thousand dreams to do.
>
> But our dreamed-of day came in field-grey.
> And took you, khakied, far away.
> 'Til broken on your shield they brought you back to me.
> And now it's I must sooth the tears,
> With loving kisses still your fears.

Terri Halpin

Terri Halpin returned to blank page and canvas upon retirement. Originally from the northern counties, she is now based in Dublin. She is the proud mother of two grown sons.

Turnover

At a woman's health day
hosted by the CWA
a young widow freshly baked
dispensed advice
with treacle cake

true love knows no hesitancy

and I returning home
critiqued a man
raw on the bone
whose abandonment issues
had married mine

and found him wanting

and left him wanting

the wily widow
picked him up
on the return

Mortaler

He came each Friday
with regularity
a plump priest
in a family saloon

took the spinstered headmistress
kneeling besotted
the space allotted
on staff room floor

a not unkindly
nor unattractive man
he heard the children's repetitive
list of sins

becalmed

another Mary

I knew a woman once
who in her dying days
so craved
a little tenderness
she crept
into the crawl space
beside her husband's bed
where his spittle
could not reach
and his drunken snores
lulled her
finally
to sleep

laid out,
he remarked, amazed,
by the beauty
of her countenance
finally erased
of all his pain

Ross Grant

Ross Grant is a lover of writing, reading, painting, nature and travel. Writing is exploring, making sense of the world. Some of her stories featured in *The Story Hatchers*, an anthology published by the Raheny Writing Group. She also contributed to 'Writing for the Contemporary', a Poetry and Postcards initiative from UNESCO Cities of Literature.

Voyage

At the age of 16 my father Michael embarked on a life-changing journey. I learned of this when I discovered his sage-green immigrant identification card in a rusty tin at the back of a cupboard. In the photograph on the card he is dressed in a smart suit. The card, similar to a luggage label, still had its ragged twine inserted around a small loop on the right-hand corner, and provided the reader with all of his personal details. On the reverse side was his immigration visa number, 21038, which was stamped by our Free State, along with the details of the Department of State of the United States and the American Consulate. His signature on the card was a reminder of how much he enjoyed writing letters.

Perhaps because he died when I was four, that card had a deep emotional significance. I could only imagine how he must have felt leaving his family, not knowing when, or if, he would return to Ireland. My last memory of him was of watching him embark on a very different journey, being carried away on a stretcher, gaunt and haggard as he left our house for the last time.

My father grew up on the family farm his own father managed, one of a large, close family of brothers and sisters. His mother looked after the poultry and had a patch close to the house where she grew vegetables and rhubarb to make jam. His Uncle Willie, his mother's brother, had invited one of his nephews or nieces to America. Willie had relocated to Syracuse, the commercial hub of New York, where work in construction was plentiful with the building of shopping centres, highways and suburban housing. They all looked forward to receiving his letters from America and to the parcels he sent over each year with clothes and luxuries shared out amongst them. Although my father had several older brothers, it was said that he chose to avail of the opportunity for adventure due to his love of reading.

The trip to Cobh was the first big journey of his life. The roads in the 1920s were primitive, the network from Tipperary to Cobh undeveloped. The long drive would have been familiar: lush, green meadows with blackberry bushes and yellow gorse on the sides of rough roads as they passed by, my father seated between his own father and mother, drinking in the sights of the cattle and hay barns for the last time before his new life began.

His sister May, who he was closest to, recalled his embarrassment and alarm when he found the brown enamel hot water-bottle used by the old relatives that his Mother had slipped into his suitcase. He didn't object to the small tan case she filled for his journey with her homemade breads, scones, fruitcake and his favourite iced cakes. May imagined he would bring with him powerful childhood memories of them helping their mother plant colourful, eye-catching lupins along the front of their house in spring, and filling the window boxes with an abundance of magenta and red geraniums in summer. My father loved the musky scent of turf burning and finding plates of hot fruit scones with golden butter melting down their sides on a rack beside the black range. He had often spoken of how much he would miss those things, and being outdoors in the meadows alongside his father, and listening to the neighbours who gathered in their small pub that sold everything from shoelaces to snuff at the front of their farmhouse. In the weeks before his departure, May was aware that he savoured his last days at home, and they laughed heartily when he revealed he was even going to miss the explosive scrapes he had with his brothers.

When he arrived at Cobh port and realised the enormity of the *SS George Washington*, he was frightened and tried desperately hard to keep his composure, but the tears flowed anyway. He later recalled the overpowering waves of emotions as he looked at his mother and father, who would be beginning their journey home without him, leaving him bereft and wondering how long it would be until they might meet again.

His steerage ticket, which cost 30 dollars, was sold without a space reservation. He had arranged to settle in for the trip with a local group. In his first letter home he recounted the misery of the four-week journey: they'd hoped at first it would take a week, but the weather was wild and stormy. As the ship sailed further out into heaving ocean, he was unable to eat much of the food he was given: stew, beef or fish. He held on to his mother's food for as long as he could but the prospect of having to eat the contents, or any food, made his sickness worse. There were times he found he couldn't quite believe that he was actually on the ship at all, out in the middle of the vast ocean with little to be seen except the astonishing spectrum of colours in the changing skies and the squalling sounds of a few wandering seagulls. He found those times wondrous between his two worlds.

When he reached Ellis Island in New York, his first glimpse of the colossal sight of the Statue of Liberty resulted in relief that he had arrived and gratitude to be going on land again. He recounted to his mother and father the details of his arrival, and of recognising his Uncle Willie, who had the same cobalt blue eyes as his mother. He felt reassured when he saw Willie, and especially by the way he held a rolled-up newspaper in one hand and slapped it several times against his thigh when he greeted him, a gesture that some of the locals used at home. He loved Willie's Ford motorcar and informed his father he was going to learn to drive. He told them about the towering buildings, the grey, white vapour oozing upwards from the drains, and being amazed at the hordes of people with little room between them on the wide streets. He settled in at Willie's two-bedroom apartment, happy that it was located on a quiet tree-lined street on the outskirts of the city centre, away from the ear-bursting city noise, where he was surprised to see stacks of coffee-stained letters Willie had retained from home on an old sideboard packed high with faded newspapers alongside old books and a radio. His room had a single bed with a wrought-iron headboard, a small desk and chair, with four strong hooks on the door to hang clothes. He relished having a bedroom to himself and told his mother to be sure to let the brothers know they could look forward to joining him eventually. He always signed off his letters telling them how much he missed them all.

In later letters he sounds to be engrossed in the new experiences he wanted to share as he became familiar with his neighbourhood, where he found himself living alongside a mishmash of people from exotic countries. He loved the character and atmosphere of the city and was astonished to see trains barrelling down Washington Street, the city's main centre, along with the crowds of shoppers, cyclists, motorists and horse-drawn carriages. He grew accustomed to the murky fug that replaced the fragrant scent of fresh air in the fields. He sampled different kinds of food: his favourite was the flapjacks with lashings of syrup. When he replaced his beloved cups of sugary tea with black coffee that tasted of molasses, his mother knew he was settling in.

He spent his early years studying and delivering milk and newspapers to support himself. He decided he wanted to get a qualification to become a draughtsman, and in the summers he worked on the building sites for experience. He built up strong friendships with fellow students, builders and neighbours. He sent postcards to his sisters of the Empire State Building and the George Washington Bridge and gave them the news of the latest swanky fashions and new soulful jazz music he encountered. His sister May framed the postcards he sent home and many years later his own children would go to see them on the sitting-room wall in her home.

His first full-time job was with a construction company building the new train station in Syracuse. By then he wanted one of his brothers to join him. This, however, was shortly after the Wall Street crash had stunned New York, and millions of people were losing their jobs and savings. Work was becoming scarce. When news came through of his father's stroke, it reignited a dread that if something worse was to happen, my father might not have the chance to see his father again. He decided he would return home, finding it heart-breaking to leave Willie and his second home, his friends and the new life he loved. His two-week return trip was not as grim as he feared. He was returning after many long years and he yearned to see and be with his family. They scarcely recognised the tall, thin, self-reliant man that greeted them, each bursting with filial love.

Dublin was in the throes of an ambitious housing programme instigated by Herbert Simms. My father decided he would set up his own business as a building contractor and live near the city. Dublin became his home as he became familiar with the buildings, streets, parks and double-decker trams. His sister May recalled that when he eventually purchased a black Ford motorcar, he would make regular trips home, giving each of his sisters a turn at the wheel. She remembered him on those visits surrounded by family with the Ford sedan in the background. His brothers often came to Dublin in response to advertisements in the *Irish Press* for jobs or to attend the football matches in Croke Park. He would have wanted them to have gone to New York; instead he always helped them out if he could.

My discovery of the sage-green immigration card had offered a path back to that watershed time for my father, and the choices that altered the place and course of his life. It also recaptured my memory of myself as a fearful four-year-old as I sensed that shift when he was no longer around. I recently came across a black-and-white photograph of Willie and the four friends my father shared those years with in Syracuse. There was a message scribbled on the back: *In remembrance of our friendship and happy days.* It was dated, and signed *Michael*. For the remainder of his life my father continued to correspond with these friends and his beloved Willie. His voyage was one of discovery, and not the lonely one I had envisioned.

I can only imagine what that voyage meant to him: it would have unlocked scarcely imaginable new experiences and emotional upheaval intermingled with loss. In the years after returning, the next course of his life began after a chance encounter with my mother. Later, of course, he had his own family, the six of us.

It is strange to think that should he have remained in New York, there would be no sister, no brothers, no me and no wonderful mother and father. To this day I am filled with astonishment at how easily I might not have been here at all.

Maria Francis

Maria Francis is a graduate of Trinity College Dublin, where she read Drama Studies and the History of Art and Architecture. She has enjoyed creative writing since she was very young, and enjoys writing poetry and plays. Maria has been part of the Ballymun Library Writers' Group since 2012, which has been a great motivator for her work.

Insightful Incisions

The world entire
As light as air
Floats into silence.
A disconnect of indentations,
Words carved in linear repose.
A cathartic release.
The flow of blood, the tear of skin,
The harmonious alliance
Between heaven and hell.
Flesh becomes porous,
Absorbing the incremental deficiencies.
The canvas cleansed,
Wounds delicately inscribed
By scarlet shards of joy
Blossoming into light with the passing of time's complicit deceit.
Losses endured,
Scriptures realigned.
As the euphoria sustains its own natural highs,
The divine absence of thought
Isolated, exquisite.

The Architect's Eulogy

In form and time
The fault lines cautiously calibrate,
Flowing through the underpass
As the rhythm and rhymes seep
Slowly into the mouth of existence, adhering to the parameters
To follow the path of least resistance.
A theory of conspiracies, of endless possibilities:
The sepia-toned approach, of daylight's dying decree
Consumed in the hallowed glow, of patriot's disease
In prayer and place.
An unholy alliance of ornate restrictions
Burrowing through the infrastructure
As the city fathers and spiritual ancestors
Inflict their rites of passage anew,
A burden of proof doctrine,
To callously subvert and subdue
Weaving its enchanted web divinely down
The stilted corridors of regret,
Embracing the shallow vows of conversation
That purge the memory of our diminishing lament.

Orla Cluff

Orla Cluff is part of the Donaghmede Library Writers' Group and has enjoyed creative writing since school. Orla is married with two kids. She has worked most of her life in finance and admin roles for relief and development charities both here and overseas, and enjoys walking, reading and writing when time allows. She is currently working on a fantasy novel for children.

The Holiday

The water swooshed dangerously close to the edge of the tin hip bath as I eased myself into the warmth of its embrace. Clothes heaped on the bare floorboards in an unruly pile. Gradually the water's heat and the roaring fire in the grate began to seep into my aching limbs, and I began to relax. I read for a few minutes from my precious copy of *Hamlet* before getting to work, scrubbing the soil from under my fingernails and sluicing the lingering smell of chicken manure from my hair. I was stepping out into my towel, warmed by the fire, when the door opened, letting in a chilly blast. Godfrey clumped across the room in stockinged feet, muddy boots already kicked off in the porch. He glanced at me shyly before attacking his own blackened fingertips with a nailbrush at the washstand. Anxiety lined his forehead.

"There's a ewe lambing in the top field."

My stomach churned. "Ciaran will take good care of her."

"She was alright the last time, I suppose. Arrah, he'll be grand. Ciaran will manage."

I pulled my fine wool travel dress over my head and observed my reflection in the wavy glass of the mirror, my usual comfortable skirt and cardigan now replaced by a neat cinched waist and an elegant hat. The scratchy garment, the chill of its silk lining, stirred up memories of previous journeys from another life. Godfrey, his suit stretched tight on his large frame, took his place beside me and we gazed at the strangers in the mirror. His eyes were bright, and a touch of colour high on his cheeks set his otherwise pasty face aglow with a boyish charm I now rarely saw. He was excited too, I knew, in spite of his apprehension about leaving. He had tackled the endless list of things to be seen to, and had prepared in his usual methodical way. Now, uncharacteristically, he patted my hip and kissed the side of my head.

We squeezed in among the dogs in my sister's sidecar and pulled our bags in after us. A tweed rug insulated my clothes from the dust. There was only my sister and her menagerie to see us off. The girls were at boarding school. Every minute of education was one chance more for them in an uncertain future: funds were scarce and they were girls. So I was happy they were there and not at home, feeding chickens.

"So you'll be wanting a lift back?" my sister scowled, her eyes squinting against the sun. A life of sparse solitude had made her dour. "Send someone up to the cottage, I'll come for you."

I looked around the empty station where she had dropped us, doubting whether there would be anyone to 'send', but I refused to allow that thought to interfere with the calm glow within. Godfrey and I were going on holiday!

Sitting opposite me on the train chugging its way out of Ennis, Godfrey's massive shoulders finally began to relax. Growing up on a prosperous farm in Meath, he would have found it hard to believe that this was the hand that life would deal him. An inheritance of a hundred acres in Clare was never going to make us rich, but a war and the depression that came after had wiped out any hope of a comfortable income for years, and maybe decades, to come.

He regarded me sadly. It was his move to my home county of Clare that had brought us together and I was happy with him. I loved our tall house overlooking the lake. I had planted copses of beech trees on the slopes and birch by the lakeside. My cousins came to tea, charmed by the everchanging vista and the Burren stretching beyond. Every spare minute I had, I painted. I was captivated by the moods of the water: sometimes pensively grey, at other times caught up in the flush celebration of Atlantic sunset. I sketched the little stone ruins that dotted the countryside and my trees grew lush in the lime soil. But I had not been raised to muck out henhouses and keep a meagrely furnished farmhouse with no servants. Godfrey felt more keenly than I the truth that, no matter how enthusiastic my relations were about our view, they returned home to much greater comfort than he could provide for me.

The spots of pink on Godfrey's cheeks were still there, I noticed, when he returned from the dining car with a tray of tea. His eyes were shining and he looked at me with a tenderness so rare it made me uneasy. Not that I didn't enjoy being the object of his affection, but I suddenly felt under pressure to respond and recently I had had little practice in expressing my emotions.

We reached Heuston Station in Dublin with its echoey babble of voices perpetually fluctuating, steam hissing and the high-pitched whistling of departing trains. I fell into step with the smartly shod throng, the cool lining of my skirt swishing against my legs as I walked. I was comfortable in this modern metropolis, despite my long absence from it. Godfrey ambled along behind, awkwardly negotiating the crowd as best as his big frame could. His ill-fitting suit, which had appeared so smart in our rural mirror, looked gauche here amongst the well-groomed Dublin commuters. I could see that his shoulders were rising with tension again and I took hold of his big hand and squeezed it tight.

Arriving at the hotel, we were greeted by impossibly elegant men in tall hats. They melted away backwards, bowing, revealing the deep pile blue carpet and the chandeliers ablaze with the magic of the electricity that was only just being brought to County Clare and had not yet reached our farm. It made the cut crystal sparkle with an intensity I had never seen before, and a warm sense of awe stayed with me as I floated through the evening. I wore a dress I had kept since my teens. The war years and the bleak life that followed had not provided much opportunity to wear such a stylish garment. Cream silk and lace trimmed, it still fitted me, the relentless activity of my life saw to that. Apart from my hands, rough from constant washing and the bitter cold, I felt entirely sophisticated.

Dinner that night was a symphony of flavours and colours and the joy of being looked after. Our every wish was attended to with discreet grace. We drank wine, and Godfrey's face, always slightly wind-burnt, shone a translucent happy pink. Inhibitions gone, he gently peeled me out of my pretty dress once we returned to our bedroom and wrapped his big hands around me. Much later that night, we slept soundly.

In the morning I rolled over and wrapped my arm around his big body – still and so very, very cold. It is the cold that I remember.

Marni J. Leonard

Marni J. Leonard contributes to the Pearse Street Library Writers' Group. She is a poet and visual artist, a seeker and explorer of the concept of truth and the complexities of human nature, both innate and constructed.

Eyjafjallajökul* 2010

The limelight chigger would not stop talking.
Her words churned Dee's anger into rage,
Hissing and spitting inside like lava gushing
At one thousand degrees centigrade.
Tightly she clenched her fist
And visualised the hit
On that silly, smile-fixated face.
Then slowly released one finger at a time,
Ending their latest round with:
"Mother always takes your side."

Hay yah feeah tlah eeaah kuh tl

52 calories/100g

.

.

..

An
Apple every
Morning. Then
Nothing until lunch
Started very young. Bea
Saw what eating had
Done to her sister
And her mum

....

Declan Geraghty

Declan Geraghty is a writer from Dublin who participates in the Ballyfermot Library Writers' Group. He's had work published in *Dublin in the Coming Times* and *From the Plough to the Stars*. He has poetry included in *The Brown Envelope Book* and *Cry of the Poor*, both of which will be released later in the year by Culture Matters. He's currently studying creative writing and cultural studies.

Brigid

She wanted a change, she said. She wanted to do something different, she said. Wanted Tommy to move in next week, she said. Sure Tommy has his own place, says I. Tommy's moving in next week, she said. But Brigid, now. Tommy's moving in next week, she said. And whatever your majesty wants, your majesty gets.

Anyway he moved in and sure he was a grand aul labourer altogether so he was, and after work we'd go back for the few spuds, d'ye see, and the pot of scald, and sure himself and herself would go up to the bedroom, and I'd fall asleep and wouldn't wake up until around seven o' clock and the News would be just over, d'ye see, and I'd be watching *Reeling in the Years* and sure the quare fella and your majesty would be still upstairs, that class of a thing.

I married herself now when she was a young one and I've a good 25 years on her still. I have the aul liatica or siatica or whatever ye jaysus call it now. I wouldn't wish it on me worst enemy, it goes down me neck, then right down the back of me arse, so the pain does. Sure I'm getting auld altogether. So I do usually sleep on the sofa. It's harder than the mattress, ye see. A lot better for the back altogether now, with my condition. Sure herself and the quare fella sleep upstairs. Not a bother on them. I won't be going up there anytime soon. Not with my condition. The pain of it is a bastard.

Anyway, I took an aul wander down to the village to get something for Brigid, it being her birthday tomorrow. The aul wander clears the head of all the nagging now, d'ye see. Sure if it was my father now he would've took the fucking stick to her but they were different times then, different altogether. Ye can't do that these days, and sure I have to get out of the house sometimes with Brigid anyway.

So I goes over to Garvan's to get a bottle of Jameson. She likes a few whiskeys with the drop of Club Orange, ye see. Well, hello Jimmy, my good man. Hello, Mr McIntee, what can I do ye for? A bottle of your finest Jameson my good man, James. How are ye keeping, Mr McIntee? Ah not bad, Jimmy, my boy, not bad at all. Jimmy can't reach the top shelf and gets a small plastic step to give him a boost to get the whiskey down. That's it, Jimmy, now you're sucking diesel, bejaysus a step and everything, sure where would ye get it.

That'll be eighteen euro, please, Mr McIntee. Out with me wallet and I hands him a twenty-euro note. I hear Big Tom is up with ye, says Jimmy. Now there's a long silence. I'm looking at him over the glasses, the aul Sellotape shiny on the bridge of the nose. And what's it to you, ye dirty nosey little shite ya? Ah no, no, Mr McIntee, ye have it all wrong, I was only making talk is all. Talk! I'll give ye talk, ya pup ya. Ah now, I didn't mean anything by it, you have me all wrong, Mr McIntee. I take a deep breath. Ye dirty swine, I remember you back in '88 or '90 when you left little Timmy Corcoran on the hill. Left him there crying in his shorts and his dirty knees and a dirty aul bastard of a Dunnes Stores bag. Yer nothing but a dirty pig, ye are. Ah no, Mr McIntee, you have it all wrong.

I turn around and storm out, slamming the door behind me as hard as I can. Fuck the lot of yis! A little bit down the village I realise I forgot the whiskey. AHHH ye! Mother of the divine Jaysus.

Back again and I open the door as quietly as I can and tip-toe back into the shop. A stunned Jimmy gulps and hands me the Jameson. I forgot the whiskey now, terrible sorry now, have a nice day now. I tip-toe back to the exit and pull the door closed ever-so-gentle on the way out.

Well, I calm meself down eventually and take a walk over to Dirty Aggie's. They're cunts in the village sometimes and sure ye do be fierce wound up some mornings as well, d'ye see, when yer a bit shook from the aul gargle the night before, that class of a thing. I wanted to get Brigid a nice vase to go with her bottle of whiskey. Dirty Aggie, Dirty Aggie and her dirty fingernails and her big aul dirty hairy chin on her. McIntee, she nods as I approach the counter. Then I walk up the back aisle. I can see her looking in the round security mirror as I glance back. I pick up a nice pink vase, so I do. To be honest now, if I was being honest with meself now, I didn't put much thought or effort into picking it.

Because Dirty Aggie was burning a hole in the back of me head, ye see. I hand the vase to Aggie. Aggie, I nod. McIntee, she murmurs with a suspicious look. Seven pound, please. Are we not in euro now, Aggie, bejaysus, 'tis no wonder you're so dear, you're still charging in pounds. You know what I mean, says the poker-faced Aggie. I paw for coins in me pocket. Aggie hates the coins. Lucky I didn't take out the wallet, it being full of notes. Anyway, I count the coins out slow. Just need to get rid of some of this shrapnel, Aggie. Me eyesight has seen better days. Have ye no notes, says Aggie. I don't, Aggie, just the coins. What's in that wallet in your pocket there, sure? Ah there's just cards in that, Aggie. Just the cards for me pensioner's bus pass to Dublin. For me appointments in James's, sure I'd be lost without it. The price of a ticket to Dublin is shockin', shockin' altogether. Shockin', I says. Dirty Aggie nods. Shocking, she says.

Anyway I hand over a ton of change and she winces looking at me fistful of coppers.

Sure look, Aggie, all you can do is smile. Aggie still poker-faced. She lays out the coppers and starts to count. It's all there, I says. No answer to that, but while she's looking down and still counting she mumbles, I hear big Tom is lodging with ye. Doing a bit of fixing and servicing. She grins at the last word. I'm looking down me nose past the crooked glasses, the Sellotape shiny. I knew exactly what she meant. Well, ye whore of a bastard wagon! Ya dirty tramp, ye! Ye filthy horrible aul one ya, I'd jaysus throw ye from a height, ya tyrant ya!

Aggie isn't easily scared but the rage surprises her. The rage and the language. She's worried now I'll kill her. I pick up a vase from the side aisle and fling it at her. I'm surprised how agile she is for an aul one, for she ducks away quickly and shouts Get out and never come back, John Paul McIntee, ye blaggard ye, ya dirty blaggard! I slam the door behind me. After going a little way up the village I look down and I'm relieved to see I still have the vase in my hand. There would've been no amount of apologising would have got me out of that one, and if I'd forgot the vase then I would've had to leave it where it was.

The trouble, d'ye see, is that the whole village knows. It isn't just the parannoya from the gargle anymore, or the reading too much into things. They know, and John Paul McIntee, the once respected GAA hero of the village, is nothing more than a laughing stock. It must have been that little two-faced yoke of a thing Collette with her big dope of a husband Harris. From when they came up last month selling the aul logs. Big grins on both their chops. I knew then they were grinning at me, the swine.

Anyway, I get back to the house, the mill looking beautiful in the distance under the summer sun. A pillar of a bygone era when there was loads of work to be had. When the place was well-off and people had salaries and pensions and houses, and could afford to live their lives without the noose of debt around their necks. When me aul da was alive. The boss, sure he was, and somehow a type of shop steward to all of his own workers. A hero, he was. I tried to keep it going for him but there just wasn't any money in it anymore. I tried everything. Every piece of energy I had I gave but it was like being made captain of a sinking ship.

I pull up a few daffodils going up the driveway and put them in the vase. Open the front door as usual, nothing different, nothing unusual about that. It's only when I get in that I realise most of the bastarding furniture is gone. The house left empty. There's no note but there doesn't need to be. The TV is still there and the sofa-bed in the sitting room.

Ah fair play to her, at least she left the telly. So I sit down and pour out a large glass of the Jameson. I put the aul vase and daffodils onto the small table beside the telly. It's as if the daffs are staring at me and smiling. Then a long sip of whiskey. Sure if I was in a bar it'd be a triple. You'd be charged a fortune for that, sure.

I'd been a bit shook from last night but I felt better straight away. I sat and stared into space waiting as my troubles melted away completely, the way only the Jameson can do it.

I start to cry. Cry hard. I hadn't cried in years. It felt good, I felt ashamed because it felt so good. I nearly felt like a sissy because it felt so good. Relief. I felt so relieved, the sheer relief of it felt like being born again, that class of a thing.

So I pour another large whiskey and the daffodils continue to smile. I switch on the TV and *Reeling in the Years* is on. All manner of war and famine flashing on and off the screen with the music of the era playing away. Then it shows the petrol shortages of the 1980s. Oh Jaysus, I remember that well. Feeling happy now. Hard to say if it's the drink or not, but it feels like a weight lifting off the aul shoulders.

Ah sure we'll get through it, so we will, says I, pouring another large one.

Michelle Leamy

Originally from Waterford City, Michelle Leamy currently lives in Blessington. She works as a librarian and, as is to be expected, loves books and spends much of her free time reading them. Michelle is a member of the Bics 'N' Brunch Writing Group, but previously met in the fantastic Kevin Street Library.

Walking Stick

Detta wrote a list of her ailments on the back of an old receipt, folded it and put it in her pocket. Before leaving the house she reached for her walking stick, rechecked her makeup in the hall mirror and called goodbye to the two Brazilians who rented the other bedrooms. They were pleasant, quiet boys who studied in the local college. She never knew if they were in or out, but she always said goodbye all the same. She was good like that.

That afternoon she left early, so she could drop into Mother's before an appointment with her doctor. The walk was always a struggle, but she was conscious of the need to keep moving, however slowly – Mother's house was a 20-minute shuffle away. Soon her right hand, the one gripping the walking stick, began to ache. Her physical deterioration was accelerating, she knew. She'd spent the previous night googling the potential conditions she was afflicted with. Unfamiliar words splayed across the white screen: osteoporosis, fibromyalgia, hypothyroidism. As far as she could tell, she had the symptoms of all three. The walking stick would soon be redundant. She envisaged herself in a wheelchair or confined to bed. It was all ahead of her.

After such a stressful night, Detta was feeling particularly lethargic. To spare her hand the effort, she did not open Mother's front door with the stiff handle but instead rapped on the window loudly with the tip of the stick. No response. She rapped again. Still nothing. Visiting Mother was always exasperating. As a lump of frustration began to rise in her throat, she heard a raspy 'It's open!' from within. Detta tried the handle, twisted it with some effort, then hobbled on through.

Mother was sitting alone in the kitchen smoking a cigarette. She sat perfectly straight and had the air of someone who was once very beautiful, although looking at her now it was impossible to tell if she ever was.

'Why didn't you answer when I knocked?' said Detta.

'You didn't knock though, did you? You tapped that dirty stick on the window. Rat-a-tat-tat. Bloody hell. It drives me nuts!'

'You drive me nuts! You know I can't stand for too long.'

'That stick won't protect you from anything, you know.' Mother stubbed out her cigarette and rose to fill the kettle. 'Tea?'

'Please.' Detta lowered herself into the kitchen chair and held the stick across her lap.

'Where are you off to with your makeup all done?'

'I've an appointment.'

'With Dr Lynch?'

'Yes.'

'A nice man, Dr Lynch. I bumped into him last week in the shopping centre.'

'Did you talk to him?'

'Just briefly.'

Detta waited, but that was her lot.

'Maybe,' said Mother, 'I should come with you when you see him?'

Detta grimaced.

'Not today,' Mother said. 'But maybe another time?'

Detta couldn't bear the thought of it. She had enough to worry about without Mother's prying and faux concern.

'No, I don't think that's a good idea," Detta said. 'I better be going or I'll be late.' Leaning on the stick, she heaved herself up and limped out of the house just as the kettle boiled.

***

'Hello, Detta.' The secretary knew her well. 'Dr Lynch is just running a few minutes behind. And there is a student with him today. Is that alright or would you prefer to be seen alone?'

The question threw Detta off balance. Nothing of the sort had happened before. The student would be inexperienced with patients like her. Then again, she suffered from an array of ailments and there was much to learn. Could she really deny a young man the opportunity to expand his medical knowledge? No, she needed to play her part in his education. With a dignified air, she let the secretary know it would not be a problem. Pleased with her decision, she took a seat in the waiting room.

Ten minutes later her name was called. Dr Lynch greeted her with his usual enthusiasm and introduced her to the student, a woman who was not much younger than Detta herself. Detta did not succeed in hiding her dismay. She'd had a terrible ordeal with a young female doctor in the past and distrusted all of them since.

'Julia will only be observing. Just act as if she isn't here,' Dr Lynch said, noting Detta's discomfort.

Julia appeared to give him a conspiratorial smile. They had obviously been discussing Detta before she came in.

'So what do you want to talk about today, Detta?'

Detta took the receipt out of her pocket and unfolded it. Her hand was shaking as she handed it to Dr Lynch. He casually glanced at it before placing it on his desk.

'Before we get to the list, and we will get to it, let's check in with how you are feeling. A few months ago, I recall, you were struggling with anxiety. How are things now?'

The anxiety was the last thing she wanted to discuss. She wanted to focus on the severity of the arthritis. There was also a persistent dull ache in her back, accompanied by a sharper pain in her lower spine. A symptom of cancer perhaps? Or sclerosis? Her memory had also been very hazy recently.

'I'd prefer to discuss the list first,' Detta said firmly.

'Sure.' He leaned forward in his chair and handed her back the receipt. 'Talk me through it.'

Detta tucked her hair behind her ears to steady herself. She tried to read from her list like a newsreader, clear and detached. When she felt her voice waver or her eyes water, she placed her hand on her belly and breathed deeply. It took all her strength not to cry out, 'Help me, for God's sake! I'm losing control of my body. It is collapsing! My world is collapsing!' But then he would start with the anxiety, the stress, the panic, the moods. All those weak words she detested.

And so she continued reading, remaining poised. She wanted Dr Lynch to treat her pain as a genuine medical issue. At least, she thought she did. If he said there was a serious condition depleting her physically, she would despair, of course. But if he disbelieved her and said there was nothing actually wrong, then she was crazy. It was either physical illness or insanity. Which was better? Which was worse? Were they both the same?

When Detta finished her recital Dr Lynch began to speak. She watched his lips opening and closing. She concentrated so hard on looking engaged that she couldn't understand anything he was saying.

'The chances that there is something seriously wrong are …'

'Okay.'

'… and I would definitely recommend decreasing the use of the …'

'Sure.'

'This is a prescription for …'

Head tilt to right.

'… good if you could talk to someone, your mother perhaps …'

Tilt left.

'… of the utmost importance that you …'

'I see.'

'I'm going to write down a number for a …'

'Thank you, doctor.'

When he finished speaking, Dr Lynch asked her did she understand everything. Detta told him she **did**. She took the paper he handed her, thanked him again and left the room. She'd forgotten about the presence of the female student; and once outside, she forgot nearly everything Dr Lynch said.

She marched towards town in a daze, striking her stick on the ground with every second step. Talk to her mother? Ha! What a help that would be! Mother would start with the moving home business again. But that house was never her home. No house inhabited by her stepfather could ever be. Even long gone, there was always the fear of his return.

The sky was darkening. Autumn's brief visit was nearly over. The pale moon was thin as a curled blade of grass. Detta could just make it out enough to curse it. Defiantly she walked through the streets, following the river into the local park. The roots from the trees stretched menacingly towards the footpath, causing its edges to rise and crumble. A young couple were kissing on a bench. She quickly averted her gaze.

Up ahead someone was walking in her direction. She squinted. The figure of a man, that much was certain. She thought she could discern in his shape the sloped shoulders, the very same oblong head. She felt dizzy, but she didn't lean on her stick: now she grasped it in both hands like a weapon. She strode on as the figure grew bigger. Now the man came into focus. It was no longer her stepfather, but he had his drunken stagger. He was scruffy, with a scar marking his left cheek.

'Give that here.' He stumbled forward and grabbed the stick.

Facing each other, they both held on tight. His hands were filthy and frail. They grappled for the stick, veering left and right. His grip began to weaken. Detta looked briefly into his eyes and saw a familiar emptiness reflected back at her.

Detta let go. 'You keep it,' she said.

She staggered backwards a step or two, regained her balance, and then ran from the darkness of the park as fast as her legs could carry her.

Belén González Granado

Belén 'Bel' González has lived in Dublin for the last six years. Originally from the south of Spain, Bel majored in Psychology and has always been particularly interested in words and telling stories that others will understand. For the last decade, prose poetry has been a continuous dance between emotions and sanity in her life. Bel is a participant in the Kevin Street Library Writers' Group.

(Con) Sequences

Unsynced
I look at myself in the mirror
and say
Tonight is the night
The night our bodies are just one
Our troubled souls anxiously touched

And then I see you
At moon's light

And all I feel is fear
A scream from within telling me you won't be enough
That I'll be blamed

So I finish my drink
Jameson on the rocks
and head back home
To an empty bed

Where I keep asking myself
What if

Sin É
Here we are
Me telling you I've met someone:
Someone new, exciting
One I don't see every day
That I get to know little by little
And how great and fresh that is
Right?

'Cause you're agreeing with me
Saying you've decided to move on
To give that girl a chance,
Her that's so troubles-free
Where there's no history

And I look at you
You look at me

We share the same corner at the bar
We keep coming closer

But here we are
Giving other people a chance

Can everyone see what I'm seeing here?
The internal fight
Knees almost touching
Hearts already touched

Another sip of Guinness
Another Saturday
Another chapter in our
– Or *my* – story of us

Mine /mʌɪn/
Tell me baby
Will you still be mine when the wine wears off?

Because I feel it too
The numbness and the crazy thoughts

Whatever your name is
I warn you not to kiss me
'Cause I'll want it all

I promise I'll let you buy me a drink
and that I'll play with my hair while cheekily smiling at you
We'll dance and fool around

Because the truth is
that I only like you when I'm drunk
And I only like me when I am not

So, tell me baby ...
Will I ever be mine?

Bob Corazza

Bob Corazza contributes to the Pearse Street Library Writers' Group.

The 'Do'

"It's been a bit of a while, darling. Jim? Yoo-hoo! Are you there behind the paper or am I talking to the back of the chair?"

"What's that, dear?"

"I'm saying it's been a while. Since we've had anyone round."

"Really? The postman was here earlier this morning, we got more of their junk mail from next door. Bloody nerve of Jackson, sending his rubbish round here."

"I mean a gathering, you know, an evening do. We haven't had anyone over since the Covid began."

"To be honest, I'm enjoying the break from my lot. How I ended up with such a bunch of misfits, I'll never know. Mind you, you've not done much better."

"Jim darling, it's not hard to see how you've ended up with a load of duds as friends. You're forever stopping to talk to every stray on the street. Yesterday, on the way to the shops, I asked if you were going to get the cat food and when you didn't answer I looked back and there you were, at the bus stop, chatting away merrily to … Who were they again?"

"I don't know. One had a Fitbit thing, so I stopped to ask about it."

"See? That's how you end up with so many desperate friends."

"That's a bit rich. Most of your lot were impossible to handle at our last do."

"Really? You didn't seem to have any difficulty handling Janine when she was leaving!"

"I was only helping her out, dear."

"Out of what, dare I ask? Anyway, a lot of my friends *do* like you, and I don't believe for a moment that you don't enjoy their company."

"A couple of them are easy-going, I'll give you that. But some of them yak away about absolutely nothing. The last time Sylvia had me up against the freezer for at least half an hour banging on about your scatter cushions. Which reminds me – I'm not sure how you manage it, but it's very awkward getting onto the couch since those cushions arrived. Next time, perhaps we could hide a few. Like, on our bed, with the other six?"

"I *like* the cushions, Jim. They add a bit of colour. And don't think I didn't see I you dropping them one by one over the back of the couch."

"Mary, we spent two months searching for a comfortable couch. If it wasn't the size, it was the button-back you didn't like, or they were too heavy looking, or the fabric was the wrong shade. When we eventually got one back here, we spent another two months hunting around for scatter cushions to hide the blasted thing under. Surely to God someone has produced a couch with scatter cushions printed on the fabric. It would save a hell of a lot of running around and make our lives a lot easier.

"Anyway, Sylvia's not the worst. It's that early-rising Veronica who takes a bit of getting used to. Does she really have to call around at the crack of dawn every morning?"

"I *like* Sylvia, Jim. And she's been very lonely since her second husband ran off with the first one."

"Basil has run off with Len? That's a pity. I was fond of Basil. And you're right, I can see how it might be an awkward time for Veronica, losing two husbands out of the blue like that."

"Yes, she so enjoys a heart-to-heart now and then."

"Now and *then*? It was every *day*, Mary, until the Covid came along. You're in the kitchen or garden fiddling around, and I had the job of answering the doorbell every time it rang. There I am, halfway through an article like this one here, Scotch eggs versus a pizza for a nutritious diet, then the doorbell goes and there she is, with that big wide toothy grin of hers. As far as I'm concerned, the Covid has been a bit of a godsend."

"Don't be so grumpy, darling. I thought you liked people calling in, sort of cheers the place up."

"Didn't actually know the place *needed* cheering up."

"It does get a bit quiet at times, Jim. As for that fiddling around, as you call it – if I didn't *fiddle around*, there would be no washing done, nothing in the fridge, nothing on the table. In fact, you're damn lucky I like fiddling, and it wouldn't hurt if you put that paper down occasionally and took up fiddling yourself."

"I fiddle."

"Of course you do. So next Saturday for a do – what do you think?"

"Not Saturday, Mary. Make it Sunday. Then those who have a job to go to can nip off early."

"Jesus, Jim, you really did get out the wrong side this morning! What's wrong with Saturday?"

"Well, if we have them round on Saturday, we lose a little of our manoeuvring time. We'll be planning all day Saturday for the soirée, then cleaning up all day Sunday. It sort of banjaxes the weekend, and I thought we'd decided to keep the weekends for ourselves."

"A do is for us both, Jim. We both invite our friends, don't we?"

"Yes, we do. It's just that last time it struck me that most of them would be happier wandering about on the funny farm."

"Like who?"

"Margery, for one. What planet did she get off? And why on earth can't she call a bread knife a bread knife instead of 'a serrated thing.' What sort of carry-on is that?"

"Jim, it was your friend Ronnie who made an issue out of that. Why he couldn't just let it go I'll never know. The fool got so agitated with Margery he fell over her dog."

"Well, there you are. What was she thinking bringing that dog of hers, the thing's a horse. Surely she remembered we had a cat."

"She loves that dog. She takes it everywhere with her."

"For an evening of drinks? And then there was all that faffing about trying to get it unstuck from the cat flap. What on earth is it, anyway?"

"A Maremmano, I think. Anyway, it's a lovely great gentle thing."

"The cat didn't think so, she shot out the room like a rocket when she saw it."

"Alright, Jim, but what about *your* friends? I was standing with Bill by the window, chatting about his troublesome neighbours and their noisy cockerels, when we saw Philip kissing that flashy car of his."

"Oh God, not that again. Philip is a complete idiot at times. I can't work out whether he's had a lobotomy or needs one. You wouldn't credit it, but he's a director of 13 companies. I guess he just finds the weekends boring. Before arriving at our do, he'd dropped into Miracle Motors on the pretext of buying a Roller, then cruised up here for a test-drive. I saw him messing with it out there. I invited him in, but he was too busy timing how fast the electric windows went up and down. I thought he'd finally lost the plot but then he challenged me to an electric-window duel with the Jag."

"Oh, for God's sake Jim, you're as daft as he is. I take it he won?"

"No, the fool couldn't wait to give me a demonstration. He leaned in to press the button and was just pulling his head out when the window shot up, catching his tie and pinning him to the top of the door. Being short, he could open the door but couldn't reach round to release himself."

"Why didn't you help?"

"Tough love, Mary. I walked round to the back garden and had a chat with Paula, I'd seen her sneaking about in the shrubbery with her secateurs."

"What a bitch! You ask a friend round for a few drinks and they rush off and start taking cuttings."

"She's a horticulturalist, Mary. What did you expect? Any more coffee there?"

"There's enough for two small cups. Shall I heat it up?"

"No, it'll be fine. Listen, you're not thinking about putting boiled sweets in the ashtrays again, are you?"

"Of course I am. It stops people smoking."

"It didn't stop Helen. She pocketed the lot and lit up. And the rest stood outside and spent the evening filling my rose beds with dog-ends. At least Mongrel McPherson doesn't smoke. Is he your new personal trainer? God, he's a hairy specimen."

"He's a bit arboreal in the chest-hair department, I'll give you that."

"It's the wide nose and sweeping forehead that gets me. He's definitely nailed the Neanderthal look. Mind you, I suppose anyone who looks like that and doesn't mind is ideal as a personal trainer or counsellor. Anyway, you fairly launched yourself at him when he stomped in. Liz said it looked as if you were trying to orally steam-clean his collar."

"I most certainly was not! And while we're on the subject, you can forget about inviting Janine. I saw you at the front door. How is it that when you hug me your hands start round my shoulders and slide to my waist but with Janine, you start at her waist and work on down?"

"It was late, my arms were tired."

"Oh? And what about earlier, when you were all over Helen?"

"Now be fair, Mary. It was a spontaneous act of natural kindness when that horse chased the cat through the kitchen. She had a cigarette in one hand and a drink in the other, what else could I do?"

"Saving the cat would have been a good start."

"Can I remind you that it was *your* friend's horse that went after Purdy and got stuck in the cat flap? And what's more, Mary, after I got finished brushing Helen down I looked up to see you and Charlie on the floor, halfway through the cat flap trying to release the brute. A damn good kick would have sent that horse on its way, but oh no, you had to get down with Charlie and push the thing through. It all looked a little too cosy from where I was standing."

"It wasn't like that at all. My watch strap snagged on a nail or something on the far side of the flap and Charlie was only trying to release it."

"Why didn't he go round outside, instead of trying to squeeze through the flap with you?"

"*I* don't know! Why don't you ask him? He's one of your misfits, after all. I admit he was a tad enthusiastic, but that was probably due to the amount of wine you poured for him. I don't know why you didn't just fill the cafetiere with wine and give him that."

"Misfits? *You* can talk. What about Lorraine, who used to wear a mask before we'd ever heard of the Covid?"

"You leave Lorraine out of it. She always had a bit of a thing about her lip. Ann tells she went in for a bit of plastic surgery and slipped into the butcher's next door by mistake, which was how she ended up with such a sausage."

"The poor thing. Only the one lip, I take it?"

"Yes, but it was a near thing, because there was a McDonald's on the other side and she could have ended up with a Big Mac. So, what about this do?"

"Is there anyone left to invite?"

"I don't suppose there is. A takeaway, then?"

"No, let's go out. This chap at the bus stop the other day swore that the new Hungarian restaurant in the High Street is top notch. I think I quite fancy a nice goulash. And if the waitresses are nice, we can always invite them back here afterwards for a do."

"Oh, Jim! Can we do karaoke?"

"They're Hungarian, Mary. They won't know the songs."

Alan O'Farrell

Originally from Tallaght, Alan O'Farrell currently lives in Ballyfermot. Prior to Covid 19 he frequently attended the writers' group in Ballyfermot library. He previously studied French and Philosophy in UCD and is currently studying data science at the National College of Ireland. This is his first published work.

The Saddest Thing I've Ever Seen

It's not something I'm sure I really saw:
A dead otter splayed on its side
In the lee of a pub at Merchant's Quay
Like some small city drunk dozing in the shade.
How it got there I'll never know:
Maybe she'd fled some madman's menagerie,
Or climbed from the parched banks of the Liffey,
Slowly emerging in the summer heat.
Or maybe it was all just a mirage,
A mysterious sign my mind needed to see.
No matter. Years later the details persist:
The shiny dark pelt, like some glossy head
Of wet human hair just washed,
The open mouth twitching skywards in death
As if pausing for thought or mustering a sneeze
And the skeletal ribs rising to a slope
To protect in vain the stilled lungs and heart.
From the window-side seat on the top deck
At first I did a double take, ashamed

To stare at such a sad and mundane scene,
This poor little fellow fallen on hard times.
But as we idled, the picture's parts began
To resolve into a more bewildering whole,
Confounding human sympathy with something
Larger and stranger.
Then we eased forward, the bus skirting
The river's banks, ferrying us homewards
To our canny, shaded certainties.

Ode to a Smoke Break
(For K.M.)

The smoker romances the smoke,
Enjoying its unhurried rise.
The lithe streams of her tokes
So graceful she's almost surprised.

Its slow ascent puts her in mind
Of her breath and the word *aspire*.
In this reverie she can be kind,
Set free from rational desire.

Dull embers creep toward the butt,
The glib world will soon call her back:
The creative hiatus must always end
With all things back on track.

Later she'll know she should try to quit
But for now her senses can stray
And wallow in the easeful drift
Of this Lethean holiday.

But, restored to her desk, she'll smile
And remember she managed to forget
During this vaporous exile
Labour's endless toil and fret.

Life's novelty shows itself true
When the smoke clears from our sight,
Familiar things becoming new
In thinning mist or shifting light.

Camillus John

Camillus John was bored and braised in Dublin. He has had work published in *The Stinging Fly, RTÉ Ten, The Lonely Crowd* and other such organs. He would also like to mention that Pats won the FAI Cup in 2014 after 62 miserable years of not winning it.

Ko-Ko-Ko

Part 1: Bird's Bop Apocalypse

Charlie Parker would have been a chin-stroking 101 years of age in 2021. Kloop. Mop. Rebop. Apocalypse. Happy birthday, with a whirlwinding flurry of breathless demisemiquavers on top.

He was Bird. And we were bird too. All three of us: Finchy, Robin and me. I was nicknamed Kestrel at the time because I once read *A Kestrel For A Knave* backwards through a trumpet for a bet. They were the eejits who gave me the moniker. Believe me. Long forgotten now. It didn't affect me at all. Just that single homicide. Water off a duck's back.

When Charlie Parker swooped down on Ballyfermot in the late 1980s, it put us into such a bodacious flap that Robin and Finchy wanted to jump out my box-bedroom window, flap their arms and fly with the bebop good news to the Moon Nightclub, which took place in Cool Steve's gaff on any Saturday his parents were out of town and had left the house in his capable jazzy hands for the evening.

We were spinning and re-spinning a Charlie Parker record I'd bought in Dolphin Discs on Henry Street for the one hundredth time. Addicted. Dizzy. But Dizzy Gillespie is a different story. I discovered Charlie Parker in the late 1980s on an alto-sax high in the clouds on an airplane to Nairobi. I was going to Kenya for the summer to do voluntary work with a group of students and teachers after raising money for it all winter, organised by a De La Salle Brother from Portlaoise called Kevin. I wonder where he is now. He looked, and held his chin, like Ornette Coleman. The airline, would you believe, supplied free headphones and a radio station to listen to while you were flying, along with a meal every two hours or so. You'd be lucky to get a green-wellied boot up your rear-end on a plane these days, let alone earphones. I tuned in during the jazz hour by happy accident. Charlie Parker's *Ko-Ko* was playing. I was flying in all senses of the word. Sucked down his rabbit hole. This stuff from the 1940s was still revolutionary, modernist and cool, cool, *cool* man. Finger-click. Dry-ice. And it led you on, if you followed Bird's trail, to the meaning of life himself: John Coltrane.

Unlike today, music in the 1980s and 1990s was still progressing and experimental. From Punk to Post-Punk to Indie to House to Rap to Hip Hop to Techno to Jungle, and all the rest too numerous to circle and highlight in screaming-out-loud yellow magic-marker. What it took classical music and art centuries to achieve, jazz did in a slick forty years, perhaps less. Finger-click. It progressed so fast to Schoenbergian dissonance and beyond to Outer Space that it's hard to believe it actually happened. Charlie Parker was the author of one of its biggest, swaggering giant leaps forward: bebop. As musicologist Ted Gioia said: 'From folk to popular to fine art.'

Charlie Parker was born in Kansas City, Missouri, on 29th August 1920, into a hard working-class life in a segregated nation. *Ko-Ko. Confirmation. Donna Lee. Ornithology. Billy's Bounce.* Just a few of the wormholes to other, better, sunnier dimensions he's left us with on earth, if you choose to stand up, turn around and leave your cave. In such circumstances, for jazz to be preserved and passed on to future generations, like most traditional music of the world, would have been a spectacular feat in itself. But to actually move it forward constantly, with an ideology of change as its beating heart, and with such intellectual pyrotechnics, was in the realm of science-fiction. Buck Rogers and Twiggy interpretive dancing on top of Star Wars' Millennium Falcon. The black working-classes were despised at the time and so was their art music, jazz. Dubbed 'degenerate'. Apparently, bebop was initially created as a barrier of entry to whites, who had taken over the more popular big band swing scene at the time. Hence bebop's fast tempos, so no one would be able to play it but themselves. No one could wear a beret and look cool, either. No one. Except bebop.

The 1980s and 1990s, as musicologists Mark Fisher and Simon Reynolds said, was a time of progressive movement forward that would soon come to an end with the X-Factorisation of an entire society into sentimental slopheads and technique idolators, which went hand-in-hand with the deterioration in people's working terms and conditions, housing and health provision, thus leaving modern music the preserve of the privileged.

But back then, with my two birds Finchy and Robin, attentively listening to Charlie Parker in my box-bedroom in Ballyer, everything seemed possible. All we had to do was jump out the window, flap our wings and fly to the moon. And do you know what? Finchy jumped and flew for thirty seconds. We all saw him. And gasped. We can still see him. He's a professor of Economics now. Forever chasin' the bird, man. Forever. Kloop. Mop. Rebop. Apocalypse.

Part 2: The Man With a Rat for a Nose

'I've been having headaches, doctor. Twenty-four-hour headaches. Car-crash headaches. For the last fifteen years. That's why I'm here. I can't stand it anymore. Please relieve my pain.'

'Mister Tweezers, you do know that you've got a rat for a nose, don't you?'

'It's not your normal shape, doctor, I grant you that. But it's not a rat. That would be ridiculous.'

'It *is* a rat, Mister Tweezers. How long has it been there? Why hasn't anyone noticed that before and removed it?'

'Why would you want to do that?'

'The headaches, Mister Tweezers. The rat is probably causing your 24-hour headaches.'

'They're low-level headaches doctor, a lot of fuzz and cloud but very little hard pain.'

'Then why did you come to me here today for a diagnosis? Because I'm diagnosing you with a rat for a nose that has to be removed. It's ruining your life.'

'The *whole* rat has to be removed? Can you not just remove his legs initially and see how that pans out? I've become emotionally attached to that Rupert on my face. It would be too much to lose him all in one go. I'm a Viking, we look after each other, this can't happen. Is there no other way?'

'When Rupert's gone, Mister Tweezers, your headaches will be no more. The world will be a lot sharper and shinier for you. You'll enjoy life much better. Fall in love. Don't you *get* that?'

'My father stamped that rat into my face when I was six years old, before he left for his exclusive tax shelter on Jelly Island. I haven't seen him since. Losing Rupert would be like losing my father all over again.'

'The headaches, Mister Tweezers. The speed-metal headaches.'

'Rupert was virtually dead after my father stamped him into my face. I ministered to that rat like a highly skilled surgeon. He's still alive-alive-o, vivaciously, as you can see. I regurgitate food to him three times daily up from my gullet. It's my whole life's work.'

'But the headaches, Mister Tweezers. And it's also now a health and safety issue for the city as a whole. I'll have to inform the authorities. Sorry, but I have to do it. I have to press this red button and scream.'

'No you won't, doctor. Because you'll have a rat for a nose too if you try to squeal on me like a filthy pig.'

The doctor picked up his phone. Tweezers bent down and produced a cage from beneath the table. He grabbed the rat, Derek, who had been squirming inside, and threw him at the doctor. As he screamed, Tweezers jumped over the table and stamped the rat expertly into the middle of the doctor's face.

Eventually, when the blood stopped gushing and the doctor was sitting back upright in his swivel chair with the beginnings of the worst headache he had ever known coalescing in his skull, he said: 'But why have you done such a cruel and obscene thing to another human being, Mister Tweezers? You've created another monster. Why? I now have a rat for a nose, just like you. And it's quite distressful.'

'You should be thanking me profusely doctor, because I stamped Derek into your face with such skill that he's still alive. I'm a very caring person. A revolutionary. An animal lover. Besides, you were going to have me arrested. I would have been sectioned. Will you write me out a prescription for a very strong painkiller now?'

The two rats looked at each other.

Part 3: The Viking's Guide To Charlie Parker's Greatest Solo

I couldn't afford a house with a proper bath anymore, one with my wife in it. These days there was always someone else I didn't want in the bath practicing Charlie Parker solos from sheet music on a stand beside the taps.

Every night at seven o'clock on the fat nose I heard the splash of someone else getting into the bath upstairs and blowing on their saxophone. Don't get me wrong, I like the sound of a saxophone as much as the next chap but I'd much prefer if it were my wife playing instead. And he wouldn't even need to play, his being in our bathroom would do me, or just even in the house. Anywhere in the vicinity. I miss him, my wife, I do. Outrageously.

But he was never in the house these days. He hasn't come back from the revolution yet. I lock all the doors when I leave the house early in the morning and go out digging but it's no use, at seven o'clock in the evening as I arrive home, tired and used, as regular as clockwork, there's always someone else, a complete stranger, in my bath. Playing Charlie Parker. What's that all about? Bebop exploded in the 1940s and 1950s, even earlier perhaps. Why weren't they rapping, hip-hopping or beat-boxing poetry in my bath instead? Charlie Parker didn't make sense in any way – although I do adore his music, and my wife was also a huge fan. *Is* a huge fan. He was the one that introduced Bird's improvisations and provocations into my head and belly in the first place, actually.

And tonight it's Valerie Valhalla from Accounting – she told me so when I asked – in my bath wearing a Viking's helmet and zipping through one of the finest Charlie Parker solos ever recorded, note for note: *Ko-Ko*.

Which is missing the point, if you ask me. She didn't/wouldn't add anything new to it herself. No improvisation. No twist or twirl of creativity as far as I could hear. Nothing from out of her own guts at all. Note for note for note for note. Had she learned nothing from his music or those that came after?

I asked her. Valerie Valhalla. But she just swivelled the question back at me while tweaking my nose. Had I, Robin, learned anything from his music? *Be twisty-twirly*, she said, standing with her hands on hips now, splashing the sheet music as she did so, soaking them in bubble bath.

Before I did my usual and frogmarched the person in the bath out the front door by the scruff so I could eat my dinner in peace and divine quiet, I bit my lip and counted to ten. Tried to come up with something.

'You know what, Valerie? My wife's name is Valerie too.'

'Now you're getting it. *Bobbity boo bop slap*.'

'And you look like him as well. In a way. It's not, is it?'

'*Skiddle dee do slap de bloop*.'

'Stop skiddling me. Please take off your Viking helmet so I can see you clearly.'

She did, and placed it on the toilet seat with a '*Moodle dee slap caboodle dee whack fol dah day*.'

'Valerie. Please come home soon from the revolution. I miss you so much. Please come home.'

Eimear Grace

Eimear Grace lives in West Dublin. She is a member of Ballyfermot Library Writers' Group and enjoys responding to written prompts at meetings. She loves to write poems, plays and novels. Eimear is currently editing her third novel and her dream is to publish all three in the near future.

My Four-Year-Old

Walking along her hand slips into mine,
She does it without saying anything.
A tiny hand that fits mine perfectly,
So small, so soft, so comfortable.
She's looking for a sense of security
in my grip, and I can offer her that:
I can keep her safe, for now anyway.

I know I'll dream of her delicate hand
for years to come, firmly rooted in mine.
When I pick her up she wraps her little
legs around me, rendering it effortless
to carry her – more supported am I
for having her straddle me, arms and legs
tight, for she's the one who provides me with
a sense of belonging and I become
the child, clinging on, feeling safe in her hold.

Basketball

My eyes won't shut
They won't stay closed
Tension travels
Down to my toes

Eyelids flicker
Bounce up and down
Endless drills
Bound and rebound

Brain pumped up
Tip off in sight
Rules of play
Pivot left, then right

I try to settle
Fall into a dream
I should meditate
Drink less caffeine

Stuck with a basketball
Pounding in my head
Blocking and dunking
Yet still in my bed

May as well get up
No peace on the bench
Get back in the game
The pressure, immense

Beneath dry, vacant eyes
Dark circles form two loops
And I know what lies ahead
Another night, shooting hoops

Brendan Shanahan

Brendan writes to prove that his future is not behind him. His writing is guided by a song entitled *I Did My Best*, written by a famous songwriter that nobody has ever heard of – Brendan Shanahan.

Bansheeism

When I arrive in Cork the Shandon Bells are ringing, proclaiming that all was well, even though it is not. Not if you're Margaret Hickey.

You probably don't know that the Shandon Bells use a fixed Ellacombe mechanism frowned upon by true-blue campanologists. Most people don't. You pick up a lot of stuff like that when you've been around for a while, and I've been around long enough to remember the crow perched on Cú Chulainn's shoulder, the blood spatter when Brian Boru was beheaded in 1014 – he was reciting the Joyful Mysteries at the time. I vividly remember the death of Joseph Mary Plunkett following his marriage to Grace Gifford. I remember Michael Collins and Éamon De Valera, too, and the roadblocks on O'Connell Street when Nelson's Pillar was blown up and the throngs came swarming around hunting for souvenirs.

I'm a banshee, you see. I've been around a long time.

The role is largely misunderstood. Misconceptions abound. I'm seen as an ogre, a portent of bad news. This is a little irritating, because I see myself as a harbinger of *good* news. It's a matter of perception. To the living, the banshee's keening sound is high-pitched and piercing. The dying hear it differently. They hear it as a deep and comforting sound as they start to slip away, a kind of meditation mantra akin to the pealing of the Shandon Bells over Cork City down through the centuries.

Of course, most people are afraid of death, and with good reason. My job is to assist them with a calm and gentle leap into the unknown. Strong encouragement is needed on occasion, but violence is only used as a last resort. Over the years I've assisted thousands of souls on their last journey. Most were uneventful.

I'll be retiring soon, and I'm looking forward to those dark, misty evenings when I can relax and watch the cosmos go by. I worry for the future of bansheeism all the same. Last I heard, the training school hadn't had any intake for decades. It was different in my day. It was hard work, certainly, achieving a wailing sound adaptable for use in all weathers: wind, rain, hail or snow. You needed a competence in high and low registers, proper breathing and concentration levels of a very high standard. A complex course, with a high attrition rate. These days it's all changed. Our habitat is under pressure. Urbanisation and 24-hour lighting have taken their toll. Noise pollution, and particularly competition from jet airplanes, is a serious problem, this in addition to the ambient background sound of cities that never sleep. High-rise buildings don't help, their funnelling of sound giving rise to echo and distortion. And don't get me started on the Shandon Bells and their fixed Ellacombe mechanism.

Anyway, I have one last call to make, which is why I'm in Cork. I'm feeling a little edgy about this assignment, and unfairly treated, if I'm honest. I was hoping for an uncomplicated final posting, but I'm here to visit Margaret Hickey, of No. 9, Wellington House, Patrick's Hill, which is a fine three-storeyed house with high ceilings and large Georgian-style windows. I've been here before, you see, and suffered a torrent of abuse. Mrs Hickey's son was dying at the time, and she was very angry and in major denial. My best attempt at keening was obliterated by verbiage never before heard in the English language, or the Irish language for that matter. A Norwegian colleague assures me that, in Norway, people are much more conservative in their use of language, and more relaxed when it comes to such matters as death. The kaleidoscopic cursing of Irish people, on the other hand, is a gift that has been passed down from generation to generation, and Mrs Hickey was outdoing herself. Her rants at the Sacred Heart hanging over the kitchen door had to be heard to be believed, and only surpassed by the threats issued against the crucifix suspended on the opposite wall.

That was all a long time ago now, and Mrs Hickey recently turned 90 years of age. I'm hoping, as I alight on the end of her bed, that with age a modicum of maturity has arrived, and that everything will run smoothly.

Unfortunately, Mrs Hickey appears to have rallied. My hopes of a swift and smooth transition have waned. To pass the time I take a wander around her house, admiring her interesting artefacts. A daguerreotype of Henry Clay hangs prominently in the sitting room. On the dressing table there's a silver tureen with an intricate design, with the surname Shanahan emblazoned on the lid, beside a photograph of Buffalo Bill. I am particularly interested in the daguerreotype, given Henry Clay's radical views on society and his possible connection to the great Muhammad Ali, aka Cassius Clay. The Shanahan tureen is a story for another day. The picture of Buffalo Bill was probably acquired at a show performed by the legendary Bill when Mrs Hickey lived in America. It has a 'BB' squiggled near the bottom.

Notably, there are no pictures of Michael Collins or Éamon De Valera or anyone else connected to the Civil War or the War of Independence. Instead there's a picture of Mrs Hickey and a man who was not her husband posing outside the Shelbourne Hotel in Dublin, dated 1939. The man looks strangely familiar: according to the information scribbled on the back of the photo, he was the half-brother of Adolf Hitler, who had been working as a waiter in the Shelbourne Hotel at the time. I wonder if Mrs Hickey would have collaborated with Hitler's plan to annex Ireland as a precursor to invading England during the Second World War.

For some reason this triggers a memory of listening to a former speech writer of President Ronald Reagan during the 1980s, when he argued for the establishment of a grand alliance between the United Kingdom, Ireland and the United States. He wasn't taken seriously at the time, largely because his speech was interrupted by his wife charging into the room shouting that their marriage was over. There was a rather embarrassing hiatus as she struggled to get the ring off her finger, but she eventually did and threw it at him. He jumped to his feet and in so doing his wig tilted sideways as he called out, "Darling!" For a man of his age he had to move very quickly to keep up with her as she stormed out through the front door and into a waiting limousine. He managed to squeeze his way into the back seat as the car drove off. Coincidentally, that event also took place in the Shelbourne Hotel.

I wonder how Mrs Hickey would view the situation in Europe now?

Would she welcome the influence of her German friends in Brussels, or would she mourn the isolationist policy adopted by England and its damaging economic consequences? Glancing at the daguerreotype, I wonder if she anchored her views in the liberal philosophy of Henry Clay, who espoused equality for all. Did she reflect on the life of Cassius Clay and his courage in challenging the status quo? Would she have been influenced by the artifice that was Buffalo Bill's legend? The answers, alas, must remain a mystery, much like the Shanahan Tureen.

On returning to Mrs Hickey's bedroom, it quickly becomes obvious that she is aware of my presence. She puts her hand to her face as if to cry: instead, she plucks out her glass eye and flings it at me. My reflexes are still good; as I duck, the glass eye flies over my head and rattles against the door where it falls to the floor and spins like a top before finally coming to rest sunny-side up.

But she had only used the eye as a diversionary tactic, because a crucifix quickly follows and strikes me on my right breast. I wail aloud in pain and fling it back at her. Now her reflexes carry the day, and with a duck of her head she avoids Jesus, who winds up embedded in the headboard up to His knees. Her false teeth are next as they spew from her mouth and rocket across the room to land on my nose with a hefty chomp. My wailing takes on a nasal quality as I swing from the chandeliers and aim a kick at her empty mouth. A bad mistake: she grabs my legs and scratches me on the backside with her false nails before banging my head against the wardrobe.

By now I'm so disorientated that I could swear her glass eye is flying around in tandem with her false teeth like bumblebees forming up to attack. I decide I have to finish her fast, and jump headlong onto the bed with my arms outstretched to grab her by the throat. At the last instant she opens her arms wide and draws me in, hugging me tightly while attempting to sing something that sounds like *The Banks of My Own Lovely Lee*.

Then she relaxes, and is gone.

Helen Feely

Born in Boyle, Co Roscommon, Helen Feely has always understood the value of female friendship, something reflected in the observational drama and feminine spirituality of her work. She hosted the Central Library Writers' Group, Ilac Centre, Dublin for a number of years, and continues to write and publish through her weekly column and one-off short stories and plays.

Women of the East Coast

South Dock stood on the fringes of the neighbourhood. Not quite city centre, not exactly Ringsend proper.

A park on the street brought the oldies, the after-Mass crew, heading to the swings for a gossip.

The afternoon brought the new mothers desperate for a friendly face. Clinging to their prams, scared as a new recruit but actively seeking company. Delighted to be out in the world but furrowed under fleece and hats, unable to unwind, to relinquish control. Unsure of anything but the fact that they needed to park the anxiety and see a friendly face. Chatting up strangers in the hope of turning them into friends.

The hospital said get out in the fresh air but with leaking nipples and a torn vagina, getting out of bed was an effort. Leaking on all fronts if you include the tears.

In the cold afternoon the teenagers arrive with basketballs. Mothers and grandmothers get up to go: too cold, too noisy. 'See youse all tomorrow.' A routine established, a pattern formed, bums-on-seats friends.

The days get shorter. The wind chill hangs around like a scalded cat, scratching and howling. Winter will be rough this year.

The oldies retreat, the Y is doing keep fit. The basketball crew have moved on, seasonal afterschool jobs and homework to do. The mothers keep up the tradition of lurking around, thankful for the familiar faces.

A new crew arrives. Darkhaired Sadhbh cloaked in swathes of moss-green velvet, bright eyes taking in the scene. The trees bend like stalks providing shade and shelter, forming a cover for nocturnal happenings.

Sadhbh is this year's scout. Find a porch, a twig, a spoon.

Vera is tasked with carrying the cauldron. She'll arrive late so as not to cause a stir.

Bit by bit the site is prepared. The wind is up and the high rough walls provide a mask. The trees are a trick of the light: the shadows they cast are seen as innocent, it's only the trees.

The hawkish women appear, greeting each other with a nod or a sound, no hugs or handshakes here. After a year's absence, they have been summoned.

The flames are fanned, the cauldron set: there is strife about. A successor is needed, for one of the tribe is heading off this year.

Sadhbh might be too young.

Vera, a long-timer, has been overlooked for years.

Sharon is the anxious type, looking for a way out. Unsure of what she signed up for, she has been hoping to disappear from this coven for years, but is unwilling to upset the status quo.

Two cannot leave at one sitting.

Rituals rejected, spells cast.

Spellman summoned the new decree: it's read aloud at midnight.

Sadhbh takes control; O'Connell takes off in a huff.

Sadhbh delivers the *salbh*: there will be no further discussion.

Halloween as a festival is rebooted, it's too bloody cold.

No more *Oíche Shamhna*, no more trick-or-treat. All Saints has moved to April 1st.

No more shapeshifting with the howling trees; no more pots or cauldrons. The next meeting will be in the High Chaparral, Irishtown Central.

Nancy Dawn

Nancy Dawn is the pseudonym of Nancy Matchton Owens, a Jewish-American from Long Island, NY, USA. She writes poems, short stories and plays. She is part of a duo that has performed from North America to Europe. Nancy graduated Emerson College in Boston with a Bachelor of Fine arts. She facilitates Ballymun Library Writers' Group and was a finalist in *Woman's Way*. Her poetry and stories have been published in various anthologies.

A quaint restaurant in Bavaria

In a quaint restaurant in Bavaria
I share a picnic bench with German grandparents
who could be carved from a painting.
His thick white hair reminds me of my late grandfather's.
She wears a golden-flower dress,
elegant with glasses and grey hair.

He smiles warmly at his granddaughter
but he is cold to me.
The girl is our uneasy alliance,
this young girl with sea-green eyes
who reminds me of Liesel in The Sound of Music.
I don't want to stare but her eyes draw me in.
I can see through them like glass.

She smiles at me and tells me there is a menu in English,
then knocks her beer against her grandpa's.

'*Prost*,' she keeps saying.
The beer is apple-juice yellow and has a frothy white head.
The sight makes me thirsty. I lick my lips.

I am sure I could live here.
Should I feel guilty for being Jewish?
Should he for being German?
The contradictions of a past that cannot be undone.
It is today and I am in love with what I see.
My dad might never understand.

The sun peeks through under the umbrella to where I sit
rendering real life a photograph in high definition,
a masterpiece in an outdoor gallery.
The cobblestones are colourful and uneven,
a real yellow-brick road.
Green shutters on the windows,
a waitress wearing an apron of red-and-black.

A cute dog appears, and I learn his name is Chico.
I reach down a closed fist to make his acquaintance,
a non-threatening gesture.
He growls.
They say dogs know.
I wonder if he is a German dog.

My better half says he wouldn't have done that
but we are different.
I can live with that.
Life is full and so is my belly
in a quaint restaurant in Bavaria.

Dean Johnston

Dean lives in Dublin with his family. He has been a member of Kevin Street Library Writers' Group since 2018. He writes poetry and short stories.

Her Night in Court

"All rise," says the clerk, "this court is now in session, the right honourable Judge Stern presiding."

Judge Stern takes his seat, unhappy to be sitting at this ungodly hour. It is, after all, 2.23am. Making clear his disdain, he reserves his steeliest glare for the defendant. A septuagenarian, Judge Stern has seen it all, and maybe at some point he'd seen enough.

"You may be seated," says the clerk. In the dimly lit courtroom, the hushed scrapings of solicitors taking their seats echo up to a whisper in the empty public gallery. Only the shallow breathing of Ms Clarke, the defendant, permeates the silence.

"Ms Clarke," says the clerk, "you are charged with one count of gross negligence. Are you ready to enter a plea?"

All eyes turn to the most uncomfortable person in the room. Although she wears a smart blouse-and-trouser combination that suggests she's a professional, she still manages to appear dishevelled. She is clearly feeling the full weight of her predicament – almost 50, she's far too young for the depth of resignation visible on her face. Beleaguered, dismayed and close to the end of her tether, she tries to utter the necessary words but the power of speech is beyond her.

"Ms Clarke?" says the clerk. "Are you ready to enter your plea?"

But Ms Clarke is paralysed by trepidation. Her legal counsel, Mrs Broad, intervenes to reassure her.

"Go ahead, dear," she says, placing an arm around Ms Clarke's shoulders.

"Not guilty … guilty … er, not guilty," says Ms Clarke in a meek voice.

"Which is it?" demands the clerk.

"Phone a friend," murmurs a member of the prosecution.

"Not guilty," says Ms Clarke in a stronger voice. "Yes, I'm sure. Not guilty." Then she deflates into the seat. If entering the plea was tough, it was a cakewalk compared to what comes next.

Mrs Broad nods her approval. A small, stout woman in her late sixties, Mrs Broad possesses motherly instincts and legal acumen in equal measure.

"Opening statements," barks Judge Stern. "Mr Black?"

The lead prosecutor stands up, long since primed for action. Mr Black is also in his seventies, and a veteran of the court. Stern yet sophisticated, he knows that if his argument fails, his supercilious look will make the point for him.

"Picture, if you will," says Mr Black, "an 80-year-old woman detached from the outside world, living alone and dependent on outside help to survive. Incapacitated by ill health, she is totally reliant on others. To this lady's credit she is a fighter and continually strives to put her best foot forward. So how did she find herself facing a life-threatening dilemma today, your Honour? She found her life threatened today," says Mr Black, emphasising the word *threatened*, "because she made the mistake of entrusting Ms Clarke to carry out an elementary errand. The errand was not carried out, and Ms Clarke's incompetence almost proved fatal.

"It is the intention of the prosecution," continues Mr Black, "to prove beyond doubt that Ms Clarke not only acted in a grossly negligent manner but did so wilfully and intentionally. We aim to prove that Ms Clarke's decision-making is a result of her negative attitude and penchant for laziness. Your Honour, this is not Ms Clarke's first rodeo. She has, as they say, previous."

"Objection!" calls out Mrs Broad. "Not relevant."

"Objection sustained," says Judge Stern. "Please stick to the facts of this case, counsellor."

"Very well," says Mr Black. "Ms Clarke will sit here tonight and try to convince us that today's events conspired against her. She may even deny any culpability whatsoever. That depends on the Ms Clarke who decides to address the court. We have medical records confirming that Ms Clarke's relationship with reality can be described as tenuous at best. As previous convictions confirm," says Mr Black, here glancing across at Mrs Broad, "her behaviour can be described as outlandish, unwarranted and even unfortunate at times. I am all about giving second chances, your Honour, but exactly how many chances does Ms Clarke expect to receive?"

"Immaterial!" calls out Mrs Broad.

"Sustained," says Judge Stern, although it's clear from his expression that Mr Black's points are striking home.

"I fully expect Mrs Broad to give myriad circumstantial reasons as to why today's events occurred," says Mr Black. "That much we can confidently expect. However, I ask that this case be judged on the rational as opposed to the emotional. There comes a point in everyone's life when they must accept responsibility for their actions, and today is that day for Ms. Clarke."

His opening argument made, Mr Black sits down. Judge Stern nods to Mrs Broad, who rises slowly from her chair, looking past the judge as she gathers her thoughts.

"Your Honour," she says, "it pains me greatly to have to stand here and respond to this charge. Not only is my client innocent but she is also of impeccable character. My hope is that the court can see through the prosecution's bluster and arrive at the verdict of innocence confirmed by the facts presented. The prosecution may be devoid of emotion; however, if life has thought me anything, it is that we cannot understand the human condition without first considering a person's emotional state. Thank you."

Mrs Broad sits down. Judge Stern turns once more to Mr Black. "The prosecution may commence."

"Your Honour, the prosecution calls Ms Clarke to the stand."

Ms Clarke slowly gets up from her seat and shuffles towards the witness box. As she sits in the chair, she takes a long, hard look at the members of the prosecution team. They are wearyingly familiar. The clerk holds out a Bible, upon which she timidly places her hand.

"Do you swear to tell the truth, the whole truth, and nothing but the truth, so help you God?"

"I do."

Mr Black leaves his seat and to stand directly in front of the witness box.

"History repeats itself, Ms Clarke. Don't you ever get tired of finding yourself in the dock?"

"I *am* tired," says Ms Clarke. "I'm sick and tired of being sick and tired."

"Well, you're not the only one. Ms Clarke, would it be fair to say that you are a failure at home, in the workplace, and in all your major relationships?"

"Objection!" calls Mrs Broad.

"Overruled," says Judge Stern. "The witness may answer."

"I *will* answer," says Ms Clarke, here addressing Mrs Broad, "because if I don't speak for myself, they will speak for me. No," she says, now speaking to Mr Black, "I am *not* a failure. My life might not have gone exactly to plan but that doesn't deem me a failure."

"I'll rephrase the question," says Mr Black. "What success have you had in life?"

"Well," says Ms Clarke, "I've done my best to be a good mother. I was a good wife, I have a degree, and I've always tried to be a good daughter."

"Let's stick to the facts, shall we? You have two children who barely speak to you, an ex-husband who would struggle to give you the time of day, a relationship with *one* of your parents, and a degree you have never used. If that's what constitutes success, we are going to have to rethink the way we look at the world."

"Success isn't easy to quantify," says Ms Clarke. "Life has a habit of getting in the way of the best laid plans, though I don't expect you to relate to that. Do your plans never derail?"

"I am not on trial here, Ms Clarke, but if I was I would back up my statements with evidence, or, failing that, logic. Time and time again, Ms Clark, you have come before this court offering nothing but feeble excuses, yet the charges keep stacking up. Coincidence, Ms Clarke, or form?"

"I have form for dealing with the likes of *you*," erupts Ms Clarke, "casting aspersions against my character to deflect away from your own inadequacies!"

"Ah, there it is," says Mr Black. "So nice of Ms Clarke's attitude to join us on the stand," he says, winking at his colleagues. "So would you say, Ms Clarke, that you are contemptuous with everyone you deal with, or just those who tell you the truth?"

"Unlike you, Mr Black, I am not a judgemental person. You call it contempt, I call it clarity. You see things in black and white, but I see shades of grey. It serves you to jump to conclusions. I look deeper for the truth."

"Very good. So how would you describe individuals who put innocent people's lives at risk?"

"You are oversimplifying what happened."

"I see. Mrs Fox's life was *not* put at risk?"

"Yes, it was. But —"

"And were you not the person that put her life at risk?"

"Yes, I was. But you're not —"

"A simple yes or no will do, Ms Clarke. Surely enough," says Mr Black, glancing at Judge Stern, "to arrive at a verdict?"

"There were mitigating circumstances," says Ms Clarke.

"With you there always are," says Mr Black. He sits down and motions to Mrs Beecham to commence her interrogation. Now in her sixties, Mrs Beecham's glamorous appearance belies her voracious appetite for dismantling witnesses.

"Can you describe in your own words," says Mrs Beecham, moving forward to stand in front of the witness box, "what happened today?"

"Two nights ago," says Ms Clarke wearily, "my next door neighbour Mrs Fox gave me a prescription to collect from the pharmacy. My plan was to collect it yesterday. Due to a manic day in work I was unable to do so. So today I was going to nip out on my lunch break and collect it. Unfortunately, just before lunch it became apparent that certain files had been misplaced in the office. As the files were required for a case pending today, the result was mayhem. The files were recovered later in the afternoon. However, this did not appease my manager, who wanted to know who was responsible. It was the day from hell. It was after five when I left the office and I knew I had to pick up something, but as I was still quite disorientated from the day's events," Ms Clarke says plaintively, "I couldn't remember what. I went to the shops hoping that I would recall what it was, but nothing came to mind. I bought a couple of things and left. It was only later, when Mrs Fox rang, that I realised my mistake."

"Part of Mrs Fox's prescription is a heart medication, correct?"

"Correct."

"And Mrs Fox's life would be at risk if she failed to take her medication. Is that true?"

"Yes."

"And you were aware of this," says Mrs Beecham, "and also that her prescription ran out yesterday?"

Ms Clarke nods.

"Just so we are totally clear," says Mrs Beecham. "You had two full days to collect a prescription that is vital to preserving your elderly neighbour's health, yet you failed to do so. What were the items you bought in the shop?"

"I don't see how that's relevant," says Ms Clarke.

"Please answer the question."

"Some chicken and pasta. And a couple of bottles of wine."

"So you didn't neglect your alcoholic needs?"

"Objection!" calls Mrs Broad.

"Sustained," says Judge Stern.

"Your honour," says Mrs Beecham, "I am simply trying to ascertain whether Ms Clarke's days are so difficult because her nights are so hard. Ms Clarke?"

"Drink isn't the problem," says Ms Clarke. "Yes, I am drinking a little more than usual, but that's stress. It's stress that's the problem, not drink."

"Either way," says Mrs Beecham, "you're failing. I would argue that it was your ineptitude that caused those files to go missing today at work.

Inept in work, inept at home, zero compassion for your elderly neighbour and hiding out at the bottom of a bottle. This is quite the picture you're painting."

"It was my mother's anniversary a couple of weeks ago," says Ms Clarke. "I always struggle around this time."

"Your mother passed five years ago. Are we to understand that you're still using your mother's death as an excuse?"

"I am not blaming my mother," says Ms Clarke, "but her anniversary does affect me greatly."

Here Mr Graham, the third member of the prosecution team, signals to Mrs Beecham, and rises to his feet as Mrs Beecham returns to her seat.

"Nobody here is debating that life is difficult, Ms Clarke," he says. "However, you seem to use adverse circumstances as an opportunity to neglect your responsibilities. We know work is not going well for you, so let's discuss your home life. I understand that your children see you as a pathetic figure, do they not?"

"Objection!" bellows Mrs Broad. "Your honour, that remark verges on slander. Does the prosecution have a free hand to make any scurrilous remark it chooses?"

"It would seem so," says Judge Stern. "Overruled, Mrs Broad. The defendant may answer."

"My relationship with my children is none of your business," Ms Clarke tells Mr Graham. "*None*."

"I'm very much afraid, Ms Clarke, that your relationship with your children, or lack thereof, serves to highlight your failings as a parent and an adult. They idolise their father, certainly, but not you. Your daughter calls you emotionally distant. Your son has told you that you embarrass him."

"I don't have as much contact with them as I'd like," says Ms Clarke, clearly taken aback by the brutality of Mr Graham's words. "But they're grown up now, they have their own lives. My ex-husband spends money on them, money I don't have. And yes, my daughter *did* say that I was emotionally distant, but at the time I was going through a melancholy time. But regardless of how she sees me, Amy will always be my be-all and end-all. And while I might have embarrassed my son in the past, I am working on turning things around. I am. This year is going to be different."

"And maybe it will be different in that you lose their respect entirely," says Mr Graham in a suave tone. "Their love is quite obviously on the wane – lose their respect and what's left? The trajectory you are on suggests you are going to become a very lonely woman. But then, you would have us believe that that is everybody else's fault, that the universe is conspiring against you. No wrongdoing on your part, of course, just an extended run of bad luck.

"My apologies," says Mr Graham, glancing up at Judge Stern, "if that sounds simplistic, almost infantile, but that's because it is. Everybody," he says, staring hard now at Ms Clarke, "and I do mean everybody, is sick of your excuses at this stage. How will you live in a world without love, Ms Clarke? Will you become even more toxic? Will your negativity seep further into the lives of those around you? Will you put more lives at risk?"

"Enough!" screams Ms Clarke. "Enough, alright? Mrs Fox got a lend of some medication, and she'll be fine until I get her prescription tomorrow. Okay? Actually, you know what? I just can't do this anymore. I can't. I'm trying my best, I really am. Just let me *breathe* for once. I *know* my life is falling apart. It's like it's happening in slow-motion and I'm watching from the side-lines. So I get it, don't you worry. It's unravelling before my eyes and I have no idea how to turn it around."

"Try starting with a shower," suggests Mrs Beecham, "and applying some make-up."

"Would you ever just shut up!" shouts Ms Clarke. "Every chance you get you're looking down your nose! You wouldn't know a problem if it jumped up and slapped you in the face." Here she turns to Mrs Broad. "I refuse to recognise this court. I'm not interested in their statements, opinions or double standards anymore. I'm just tired, so, so tired."

"Yes, well," says Mr Graham, "constructing and maintaining a web of deceit can be very tiring."

"And how would *you* know?" demands Ms Clarke. "You were never *there*, Graham! You were never there! If they had an Absent Father of the Year award, you'd have taken it home every year, that is if you ever bothered to go home. But you're here tonight, alright. Oh yes, *now* you're here."

"Order!" calls Judge Stern, banging his gavel. "There will be order in this court!"

"You can *stick* your order!" bawls Ms Clarke, who is by now in floods of tears. Suddenly Mrs Broad rises from her seat and strides to the witness box. "Sorry, love," she says, "but it's for your own good." Then she slaps Ms Clarke smartly on the cheek. "Alice?" she whispers. "Alice, darling, it's nearly three in the morning and you're up for seven o'clock. You really need to get to bed."

"Objection!" calls Mr Black. "We're not finished with the witness."

"Oh give it a break, Bill," says Mrs Broad. "Let your daughter rest, for God's sake."

Here Judge Stern bangs his gavel again. "This court will recess until morning."

"Well," says Mr Black, "let her have a good long look at herself between now and then. We'll pick this up again in the shower first thing."

"It's okay, Nanna," says Ms Clarke as Mrs Broad is about to reply. "Dad never could let it go."

"Tomorrow is another day, love," says Mrs Broad, "and you need to sleep. Your father, your husband and that bitch from work can all wait until tomorrow."

Alice opens one eye. She's on the couch, the sitting room dimly lit and cold. Her phone vibrates again. A text, from Amy.

Hi Mam, this hen night's going to go all night. I might call around for an early cuppa before you go to work. Feels like we haven't talked in forever. xx A

Alice places the phone against her heart and smiles through the tears. In the back of her mind she hears Mrs Broad address Judge Stern: "The defence calls Ms Amy Clarke to the stand." And with those words the prosecution team – Mr Black, Mr Graham, even Mrs Beecham – start to blur out of focus, and dissipate like so much smoke on the breeze.

Michael Ryan

Michael Ryan was born in a small rural townland, Commonaline, Co. Tipperary. He was educated in Commonaline NS, Doon CBS, Co. Limerick, and U.C.D., Earlsfort Terrace, now the home of our National Concert Hall. Michael spent 36 years teaching in The Abbey CBS in Tipperary Town, serving 10 years as Principal there. On retirement Michael got involved with, and visited, Providence, a school for under-privileged children in north-east India. He joined the Kevin Street Library Writers' Group five years ago, under the direction of the late Orla Heney.

All Things Seem Possible in May

All things might seem possible to you in May – or in any other month, for that matter. 'Good luck to you,' I say, 'and more power to your elbow.' The grass may grow, the flowers may bloom, the lambs and calves may frisk and frolic in the fields, but things do not work out for me in quite the same manner.

There are so many aspects of life in which I am incompetent that there are very few left at which I can excel, even in May, the month of hope and expectation. Technology has always instilled such fear in me that I am compelled to call the neighbours if I wish to have a nail driven into a wall in the garage. Machinery, including cars and lawnmowers, 'go' when they are asked or else remain stationary until the engineers or mechanics arrive to set matters right. Given that I always encountered difficulties when I had youth as an ally, what do you expect of me today? Not a lot, you might venture to say, and rightly so.

Still, ineptitude has its uses. Because I have sold and continue to market myself as the perfect incompetent, nobody expects me to come up with the solution to anything. They know that I won't know, so they seek the assistance of somebody else, someone capable and energetic and enthusiastic. That suits me fine. I am no longer out to impress, so I am never disappointed when I am overlooked for the demanding job that requires know-how and expertise as well as huge amounts of precious time and industry. In fact, I am very pleased to have found the perfect means of escape.

Growing up on a country farm in the 1950s, I was given myriads of mountains to climb. Father wasn't a patient man. He could often be heard commenting, when a job was not satisfactorily completed, 'Wisha will you dash it on, sure you're NO good!' In a way he was right. I never managed to efficiently perform tasks I didn't like. Perhaps it was an innate tendency for indolence that inspired me, if inspired isn't too strong a word. Whether it was milking cows, tramming hay or thinning turnips, I was a dead loss. On the other hand, if I were sent to the village for the messages, or to the farthest field to fetch the calves, I was in my element. Then I could indulge my imagination, commune with nature and live in my world of dreams, temporarily at least. My reputation as a farmer was suspect but I was sought out for company, my conversation enjoyed. I became what they call today a 'people person'.

At school I managed to get through the demands of study, although not quite as well as an elder sibling, who was known as Joan Genius. I preferred hurling, so I was neither disturbed nor jealous when father complained of my limited enthusiasm with yet another 'Why, in God's name, can't you be more like your sister?', for I had no inclination to be so.

Life moved on and I found myself heading an institution of over 500 members. I think I was reasonably successful, although this was due more due to my talent for observation and delegation than any exceptional ability on my part. I managed to get those on my side who were willing and capable, and I positioned and empowered them to employ and maximize *their* talent. I gave them fulsome affirmation of their achievements while luxuriating in the knowledge that things were being done well. Imagine that. And you thought that I couldn't do anything.

I am rarely under pressure nowadays. Instead I see others flying around and fussing over what appear to me to be simple jobs. The experts, you see, have an inordinate fear of failure and can never admit to being in error. Even when they do make a mistake, they feel obliged to cover it up until they can manage to steal a couple of hours to sort things out. On the other hand, when I make a mistake – which happens quite frequently – I allow it to be seen as an affirmation of my abject inability. Furthermore, I am not likely to wade in to criticise those who did a similar job at some time in the distant past. My philosophy of *T'will do* has stood me in good stead over the years. Nobody is surprised or disappointed at my failures, and I am, on many occasions, the beneficiary of benign condescension. I don't care. I seem to have found the best of both worlds, so I won't be shifting my position for a while yet.

Only one fear remains. I dread the occasion when someone calls my bluff and compels me to undertake and complete a difficult task at which I accidentally succeed. I must be careful lest I allow myself to be hoodwinked into doing what others are only too glad to do for me.

I need my limited energy for better things. For the imagining, the dreaming, the communing with the world. After all, being a 'people person' is not a career, but a vocation.

Patricia Kane

Patricia Kane came to writing late in life. She took creative writing courses in the Irish Writers Centre and some on-line. She has a degree in Celtic Studies and likes to find ways to inject some of our ancient ways into her writing. She is now part of the Ballyfermot Library Writers' Group and has enjoyed seeing some of her pieces published with the group.

The Storytellers

MacElliott had the words
To please the King
With stories ancient and aged,
Yet still vibrant and fresh
To find a home
In every listener's heart.
MacElliott treasured the words
From the people long ago,
Whose lives were filled
With gods good and bold.
Giants, one-eyed and two,
Heroes like Cú Chulainn
And the rebel-rouser
Fionn MacCumhaill.

MacElliott's command of the words
Never would be outdone
But they did not solve his problem
Of not fathering a son.

This storyteller to the King
Had a female child,
One daughter for his kin.
No law in the land allowed her to be
A storyteller, poet or *filí*.
MacElliott was allowed a servant
So he kept her by his side
Always present, always listening:
But the power of his words
Could not stop MacElliott from wrinkling.
Still his daughter stayed by him
At every royal feast and meeting.
On one such royal occasion
MacElliott spoke the words
Casting doubt on the King's heroic past.
The words insinuated that
The rebel-rouser Fionn MacCumhaill
Sat unchallenged next to the King,
By law a place reserved for close family.

The King was furious
At such a slight.
He ordered his guards
To take MacElliott
And throw him in a bog that very night.
But MacElliott's daughter stepped forward
And in a sure and certain voice, she said:
"You did not let my father finish
The words that would explain.
Your family were not cowards, Sir,

For they shared a noble kin
With Fionn the heroic rebel,
Renowned trickster of the northern giants."

The guards paused
Still holding MacElliott tight.
The king smiled, beckoned the daughter forward
And praised her for the words so right.
MacElliott twisted out of his bonds
To stand by his daughter, truly bright.
An idea grew, and bloomed
And would not stay quiet.
MacElliott pressed the king to listen
To the wisdom of his words:
Being a King of such superior strength
He could change the law if he wished,
And make his daughter an apprentice *filí*.
Then he would have the advantage
Over all the other Kings
By having two storytellers, poets and *filí*.

So it was
From that day forth:
MacElliott and daughter
Master and apprentice.
Roaming the kingdom
Telling tales of gods good and bold, and
giants, one-eyed and two,
And giving life to our heroes,
Cú Chulainn and Fionn MacCumhaill.

Helen Sullivan

Helen joined the Ballymun Writers Group in September 2017. Her short story *The Cottage That Wasn't a Cottage* was published in *The Flying Superhero Clothes Horse*. She also has a short story, *St. Michan's Mummy*, published in *Mustang Bally*, written in collaboration with Ballymun Library Writers' Group.

The Song of the Sea

The soldier marched on through the windswept fields. Neither hurried nor slow, he trudged by thistle and dandelion heading for a destination unknown. He was weary now, his weapons weighing heavily. A thin sweat coated his mud-slicked hair, sticking his clothes to his skin.

He paused for a moment, turning to see how far he had travelled. A sharp breeze whipped across his face, and he was glad of its cool passage. While he mopped his brow he gazed back along the trail and saw that he was utterly alone, that only one set of footprints could be seen.

He and his comrades had been intruders in this land. It was no surprise then that it had not made them welcome, that it offered no sign to say from where he had come, nor any indication of where he was going. Somehow he knew that he needed none. His journey was at the beck of an ocean's call that carried on the wind.

While he listened to the song of the waves he tried to recall how he had become separated from his company, but his mind offered him no images nor remembrance. Instead there was a growing awareness that a strange feeling had taken root deep inside, a sense that his solitude was now pressing upon him, with the weight of an open sea.

Throughout there was silence and a quietness that was not at peace. From end to end the silence buried beneath the fields he travelled, a silence woven of claws, a quiet that bored into his flesh, into his marrow. His every nerve screamed. Somewhere within him was an apprehension that betrayed a life once lived beyond this land, where solitude had been his companion.

It seemed as if he had only stood pondering for the briefest of moments but when he resumed his journey darkness had swooped in and stolen the light from the day. Now the heavens were empty and as dark as the land. With no stars to navigate by, the soldier allowed his fear to rise up, to overcome him and shut out the sea's guidance. He trudged on, strides slow and feet unsteady, struck with a blindness that left only the sound of the waves to guide him. But though he no longer knew it, he had once been a man of the sea. The life of a fisherman was rooted in his soul, and so he did without thought what his father had taught him, what his father's father had done: he faced the sky, until he heard the ocean's call.

Now he marched forward to a soldier's rhythm, steady and sure and heedless to the fact that this land was not prepared to free him. His movements were seen as wilful ignorance and stirred the uneasy silence that swelled into a cry louder than the ocean's call: 'This land is not of yours, nor is it the land of your father's.' These words the soldier heard, and he knew them to be true. This was the land of shadows, where days, hours and minutes all merged into one. A land that offered no escape for those unlucky to find themselves astray.

He marched on. A hunger now burrowing deep and entwining itself around his entrails. He knew it was not a hunger for substance, but a desire to reach his journey's end. In his haste the soldier drifted from his path. He stumbled over an unseen tuffet of grass and went crashing to the ground. The land rose to meet him, for beneath the soil the unseen eagerly scrambled to claim the newcomer. But the soldier had long since proven himself a fighter, and resisted.

Thus the unseen called down winds that slanted in from the south and rain that fell in sheets. Its edges sharpened with fingers of ice that nicked and chilled his skin. And it was then that the soldier saw the unseen, who took the form of grey shadows. For the dead were no longer subdued.

They twisted and writhed through the wind and rain, weaving their way towards their prize. Their cry a repulsive vibrating that drowned out the song of the sea. It was this that gave flight to the soldier's feet, who rose and ran as fast as the land would allow, trying to make sense of it all until finally his persistence yielded an image.

Memory was a flash of light in which he glimpsed the sightless eyes of his comrades and heard their pitiful cries, and those whom he had sent to this land of death. For with his remembrance came knowledge of his surroundings. He was in the overlays of the spirit-world, where the grey shadows had judged him by his final actions. Sentence had been passed upon the soldier; he was to be held in the arms of the accursed.

But his soul knew his eternal rest was not to be spent with the shadows that shrouded themselves and hid from the light. His slumber was to be in a place decreed by his ancestors on his first intake of breath. With this understanding he leaned into the wind and found the rain had lent a softness to the ground. His weapons weighed even more heavily now, and he felt his feet being sucked into the mud. Stringy roots took hold of his ankles, and the grey fiends rejoiced when they saw the soldier had become anchored to the land. They screamed at the newcomer that had dared to attempt his leaving: 'For you there is no escape!'

With that, the young soldier quickly removed the weapons that had grated against his conscience when he had grasped them for the first time. A lightness flowed through his body and he ran as fast as the soft earth would allow. The winds wailed with the strength of a hurricane and placed a shoulder to block his flight. But the determined soldier pushed back. For in the distance a dim light had appeared, which gave him strength to do battle once again.

As the song of the grey fiends continued to chant their warning, the soldier locked horns with the wind. The two tussled and grappled, but it was the wind that wearied first and allowed him to pass. He fled towards the light with the wrath of the fiends pealing on the air, a noise he knew no living voice ever sounded. It followed him through the darkness until he reached the place of the light. A farmhouse that lay in ruin.

Exhausted and short of breath, the soldier passed through a wooden gate and headed towards a door. At the approach of his footsteps it opened, and he knew it had been with the help of no human hand. Unwilling to undertake another challenge he faltered, but with the grey fiends at his back he had little choice.

He stepped into a room that was empty save for two wooden chairs placed in front of a fireplace, the embers of a fire in its grate. A black raven perched in its faint glow. There was a familiar scent lying heavy on the air, a sickly odour the soldier had become accustomed to, one he would never forget: the stench of decaying flesh. The raven twisted his head and fixed him with its cold stare. The soldier gazed back with the same intensity, a challenge that caused the raven to screech two loud caws in warning. A caution that the soldier heeded before turning away.

For the soldier was now eyeing the dying embers, which were barely a glow. He considered them for a moment and his suspicions grew. Could they really have been the source of the light that had drawn him there? He was wary too as to why the relentless grey fiends had not followed him inside. And it was while he was wondering his eyes returned to the two chairs, where he discovered that a soul not seen before had appeared.

The soul seemed shrouded, blanketed by the dark. The soldier stared hard into the shadows, discerning twisted shoulders and fingers that were no more than bone busily working the dying cinders with a stick. It had the appearance of being an old man.

The soldier could see no reason for the soul's working of the dying cinders. For it gave no rise to a spark and nor did it extinguish. He understood the soul's doings were not of this land but derived from a remembrance of a life once lived. He thought perhaps the old man was to be his guide, and that he would be the one to disclose the answers he sought. For the soldier had not yet realised that this land was not his final deliverance. He had not yet realised that the farmhouse itself had been spun by the grey shadows and woven to stand in the way of the soldier's truth and acceptance.

The old man used his stick to tap several times upon the second chair, encouraging the soldier to take a seat. When the soldier finally sat, the raven cawed once more, knowing that the old man itched to trail his bony finger upon the soldier and claim this worthy prize.

For the old man was the Black Prince. And the Black Prince could tell that the soldier's soul was not foul or depraved, only slightly stained by the blemishes it had gathered along its way. This knowledge lent a smile to his lips, a smile that rendered his face ugly. It was an ugliness borne straight from the bowels of the earth and when brought into being stripped away a man's humanity. An ugliness the soldier recognized as an echo from his own past, his own end. Suddenly he found himself fastened to the chair, whereupon the pupils of the Black Prince's eyes dilated and grew in size.

In the deep abyss of the Black Prince's eye, the soldier saw a figure appear. He leaned forward and saw himself being taken to a land far from his own, and he watched himself hack a path that was lacking in mercy. At this, the soldier cried out in shame.

He begged for forgiveness when he saw his face sprayed with blood and spittle. When he saw all the terrible things he had done in battle. A sudden wrenching tore at everything good within him. Unable to take any more, the soldier turned his face away, but not before he had seen his own flesh and bone strewn across a battlefield that was no longer green but crimson. He believed himself to be fated to hell, and he began to let go of the call of the sea.

The soldier turned back to the Black Prince, whose smile grew as he sensed victory. Too quickly, however; with one crashing wave, the sea sent forth a faint spume of spray that misted across the Black Prince's eye. 'Turn away!' he screamed at the soldier, but it was too late. The soldier had heard the sea's call, which landed with a kiss of salt on his lips. He found himself staring at a boat that had appeared amidst the dark waters of the Black Prince's eye, and he watched himself cast his nets.

His soul rejoiced, and above the roar of the waves the soldier heard the voice of his father: 'This is not where you belong; your end is to be with your kinsmen now passed over to the sea.' At once, the threads of the grey shadows' cobweb fell away.

The soldier saw that he had once been a righteous man. That the short life he had lived as a soldier had forced him down a path that was not of his own making. That death had taken him before forgiveness could come. That at his final breath he had condemned himself for the loss he had taken from others. It was then that the soldier gave thanks to his soul, which had known its true value and had not abandoned its longing to rest in the briny sea.

With that, the soldier sprang to his feet, as did the old man, who blocked and filled the space. In the darkness of the night the Black Prince reached for the soul that had strayed onto his plains. But his action brought a thunderous roar from the ocean. A mighty wave arose and swept the farmhouse to its shore, where it summoned the Black Prince to its edge.

'Old man!' bellowed the sea. 'I have watched this soul wander through the land of shadows. It has never resigned itself to this place but has been unwavering in its desire to rest in the sea. And even though you tried to disguise its true destiny, it still claimed his right of redemption. It is time for you to unbind your claws and set it free, your claim has ended. This soul is not yours for the taking!'

The Black Prince knew the soul had been a seeker of light. That it had earned its birth-right. With his entitlement lost, the Black Prince took a final lingering glance at the soul, before he and his grey shadows turned and were lost once more in the wind and the rain.

And as they disappeared back into their accursed land, the soldier felt a ripple of water beneath his feet. A sea breeze came and embraced him, then the ocean heaved and carried him away into its depths.

Dominic Lavin

Dominic Lavin is a teacher, poet, and short story writer, currently writing his debut novel. With nearly a decade of writing experience, he has developed a unique writing style, blending humour with tragedy. He completed a creative writing module as part of his Arts degree. He works from his home in Clarehall, Dublin, every chance he gets. He refuses to keep a pet, in case it eats his work.

April

You cry your tears at this time of year
before the last veil of darkness fades
while the clamour of children are near
and angry madams scolding their maids.
Your chilly cough blows in from the west
like a sharp arrow stabbing the bone
becoming a stinging pain and a pest
and its tune, is a desperate moan.
The fury of your presence is bold
biting a trail through every day
while you scuffle with time for a hold
of the moment before the first ray.
Ah … God's clock can't freeze for a minute
 the wheels of time will trundle on
and cries from the lark and the linnet
 signifies some time already gone …

And so, your ferocious face of ice
Begins to slowly lose its firm grip
And is switched for a smile of entice
from the curve of your lilac lips.
Your dark side gradually shows more light
And your heart of stone glistens and glows
While the fire from your body ignites
Each crevice, corner and all purple toes.

Geraldine Moroney

Geraldine Moroney is a long-time member and co-ordinator of the Raheny Library Writers' Group. She fell in love with books at a young age and moved from reading to writing her own stories when she joined the group. She achieved a long held dream when she edited and published two short stories in an anthology of Raheny writers work called *The Story Hatchers*. Geraldine is passionate about writing and writes daily.

Annie Finds a Life

My library card was still on the mantlepiece. Not the ticket itself, of course, but a card that either me Ma or Da have to sign so I could borrow books. It looked so lonely up there, forgotten, but not by me. I stood on the fender and reached up to take it down, hoping that if I had it in my hand Ma might sign it for me and I'd be able to go with Connie.

Connie, me cousin, who got the card for me and said if I got it signed she'd bring me to the library today to get my ticket.

"Jaysus, what are you doing standing there so near the fire?" Ma said. "Get down before you burn yourself. That's all I need!"

With that Tommie and Shamie came tumbling into the room fighting over a toy soldier or something. Ma told them to stop all that noise or they'd wake the baby and she'd just got him to sleep. The next thing there was a cry from the bedroom and Ma had to go back in to see to the baby, as he'd started to cough. He always had a cough. That was the end of getting my card signed, I thought.

But then me Nan arrived in. "It might never happen," she said, after seeing my expression. I told her it already had. I couldn't get me card signed and go with Connie to get a ticket and borrow books from the library. So Nan took the card out of my hand and read it, then told me to see if there was a biro in the all-sorts drawer in the kitchen dresser. Now that I was eight I could reach that drawer and luckily I found a biro, and one of my hairbands, under all the bits of twine and folded brown paper.

"I'll sign the form for ye," she said.

"But you're not me mam."

"Well, I'm Mrs E. O'Toole and your Ma is Mrs E. O'Toole, so if I sign it it'll seem as if your Ma did and who will know?"

I would, I thought. Me Nan was Edith and me Ma was Elsie, and I wasn't sure about it at all.

"But that's a fib and you're always telling me not to tell fibs," I said, worried that I'd have to tell the priest about this the next time I went to confession. I really wanted that card signed, though.

"It's *not* a fib. Now do you want the card signed or not?"

"Yes, please." She wrote her name on it and just then Connie arrived at our flat, wanting to know if I was ready and to come on as she hadn't all day.

I asked her did she know that grownups told fibs and she said yeah, all the time. She told me that *she* was telling a kind of fib by bringing me to the library, because she was going to leave me there and then go and see her fella who worked in the butchers. If she didn't bring me, she'd have to bring some of her brothers and sisters with her, and they'd tell her Ma she had a fella. Her Ma thought she was too young at sixteen to be going steady with a fella. She said to hurry up.

We walked quickly down the length of the flats. I looked back at our block and it seemed so far away. I'd never been down this end before, as we usually went out the gates beside our block. Connie lived in the same block as me, only on the veranda above us. These flats seemed huge as there were blocks of flats on either side while our block looked down onto the square and there was space to play.

The sights and the sounds were the same, though. Boiled cabbage, smelly nappies, carbolic soap and Brasso. I couldn't get the awful smell of Jeyes Fluid out of me nose. Normally it was used all round on shared walkways, and verandas after a heavy Saturday night in the pub. It washed away the puke and piss. I hated the smell of it, it clung to me clothes and hair and took days to go away.

As I walked along I heard the flat dwellers calling to each other across verandas in friendly, and not so friendly, voices. Kids games and their names were called out at full volume, as husbands and wives noisily squared up to each other. Rubbish clattered down the three floors of the rubbish chutes. A coalman or a dustman might be calling out to signal their arrival, although the rag-and-bone man was the biggest draw for children, with coloured windmills and brightly coloured balloons tied to his cart. I always thought he looked like the Pied Piper of Hamelin as crowds of kids followed him around the square. I even thought I could hear a cry of a new-born baby, or the wails and cries at a sudden death. Yes, I thought, it sounds just like our block.

Then we turned out of the flats and onto Pearse Street. When we reached the imposing stone building of the library, I stopped dead at the large doors. They were huge and terrifying. I wasn't sure that I could go through them, as I imagined them closing over unexpectedly, and that I'd be squashed between them.

"Now what's wrong?" Connie wanted to know as she took my hand and pulled me again. "Come on, hurry up will ye? I'll hardly have time to see Jimmy if you keep this up," she hissed as she pushed me through the doors.

I couldn't believe my eyes. There were *thousands* of books, all sorts and all sizes. Row after row of them, and I could borrow three of them at one time. I stopped again, just inside the door to take it all in, but then Connie grabbed me again. I nearly fell, and I made a loud scraping noise in that quiet space.

"Jaysus, will ye shut up or you'll get us thrown out," said Connie.

"You *shoved* me," I hissed back. A cross-looking librarian pushed her glasses up on her nose, placed her hands on her big wooden desk and told us to be quiet or she'd have to put us out. But I was not about to let that happen, not when I'd come this far.

"Go on and meet that fella. I'll be okay. I'll wait here for ye to come back, but don't be too long." Connie didn't wait to be told again.

I looked up and around the space: it seemed to go on and on. The ceiling was high up in the air. It reminded me of the time I went to a special mass in a cathedral with me Da. That church was enormous and even me Da, a big tall man, seemed very small in all that space. I felt tiny.

I looked around at shelf after shelf of books. I was afraid to touch them. I had the giddies in me belly, like when I was excited, but then it began to creep up inside me and I thought it might burst out as a fit of giggles or tears. I didn't want that to happen. I was afraid I'd be put out. Anyway, I was a big girl, I was eight.

Oh! I'd have to go and give my signed card to that cross librarian. She hadn't looked happy at all, sitting behind her big desk. I thought it was the same height as our dinner table, and I had to reach up to take things off it when I helped Ma with the dishes after dinner. But when I looked again she wasn't there anymore, it was another librarian, one with smiley eyes. I handed her the card.

"Welcome to the library," she said quietly. "I hope you'll enjoy it and that you're ready for lots of adventures."

"You mean girls can have adventures too?" My eyes nearly popped out of my head with happiness.

"Oh, there's all sorts of adventures to be had in books and you look like the sort of girl that will be able to find them. If you come with me I'll show you where they are."

"What sort of adventures?" I asked. "Are they in foreign lands, with jungles and swamps and strange animals? Do they have bows-and-arrows and cook strange food over fires or did they live in houses made from branches of the trees in the jungle and do they wear animal skins?"

The librarian's eyes smiled again as she said yes. I couldn't believe my luck that an adult would let me ask all those questions. Normally I was told by me Ma to stop with all the questions, she was too busy, and I was to ask me Da when he came home. But he was always too tired.

Then the librarian asked if I would like to read about Ireland when it was an older land and our people a different people. I didn't trust myself to speak, so I nodded in reply as she brought me over to books on folklore and introduced me to another world. Then she left me to read.

I found a tale about Brigid, not the saint but the daughter of a goddess. Jaysus! Goddesses! I thought there were only men gods.

I read on. Brigid was the daughter Morrigan, a queen of the Tuatha De Danann and the goddess of war and fate. A goddess of war! I couldn't believe what I was reading. I read on and discovered that Brigid was a Celtic goddess of healing. Oh! I could pray to her to heal the baby of his cough and then Ma mightn't be so tired all the time.

On the next page I found another goddess, Danu. The Tuatha De Danann were known as her people. According to the tale, Danu saw that her exiled people were scattered. She promised to gather them together as a tribe, bring them back to Ireland and teach them to prosper and get back to their former strength if they followed her.

Again I closed my eyes and pictured people here and there, in France and England and even Spain. This wonderful, beautiful woman, Danu, calls to them. I see them getting into long boats with big oars and they row after her. She guides them through misty seas with special lights until they get to Ireland. When they land, they gather around bonfires. She teaches them about the land, how to mind it and make things grow. I am sitting with them, listening. I smell logs burning and the fire crackling in the hearth. Danu picks up a stick and begins to draw the sun, moon and stars, then the land with its people and animals. She teaches them special magical ways. I lean forward to listen, but all I hear is, "I'm afraid the library is closing shortly."

It's the librarian with the smiley eyes. She asks if I want to take the books on folklore home. I do.

"You bring them up to the desk and I'll stamp them for you," she says. As she leans over the desk, putting the books into my hands, she smiles. "Come again soon."

"I will, and thank you. I'll be back soon."

Outside, waiting for Connie, I stand in front of the library doors with three borrowed books under my arms, delighted with myself and the life I've found here.

Sheila Keegan Groome

Writer and Dublin native, Sheila Keegan Groome lives on the south side of the city. Sheila facilitates the Pearse Street Library Writers' Group in support of local writers. Sheila has published a collection of non-fiction books taking her readers through the seasons. This is Sheila's first venture into fiction.

Stand Fast

It was the red shoes that first caught my eye – *stilettos just don't work in puddles, sister*, I advised from my window perch high above the busy street. It was only then that I realised who was wearing them: Miss Shiny, from all those years ago. Miss Shiny Shelley Patterson, who could have done with a bit of Mr Sheen right then, what with all the rain and her mascara streaming down her face. Not that she seemed bothered. Onward she ploughed, determined to reach her destination, which, it transpired, was the bookies on the corner.

Don't judge me. It was a Tuesday. Not Monday, just after the weekend; not Wednesday or Thursday, with the weekend on the way. Just another damp and dreary Tuesday. I can hardly be blamed for staring out the window. No one needs help jazzing up their CV on a cold and rainy Tuesday. It was so long since my phone had rung that a spider had woven a web across the office landline.

So I reached for my binoculars. Binoculars, yes, for my keen interest in opera. I'd had to get rid of the telescope after the dinkies in the apartment opposite complained. I mean, really, close the blinds. It's a city.

By the time I got the binoculars focused on the bookies, a man had got himself jammed in the electronic doors trying to bundle through a pram and blown-out umbrella. And there she was, betting slip in one hand, a takeout coffee in the other – a reusable cup, of course; very green of her – and grimacing at a monitor as the tiny horses went racing by. Seconds later her shoulders slumped, and she crumpled the betting slip. She disappeared from my line of sight, and then reappeared about a minute later, when the little drama played out exactly the same way. It became hypnotic. I couldn't tell you how long I sat there glued to the binoculars, but the sky had begun to clear when she eventually re-emerged and began stalking back up the street in those three-inch stilettos.

I wondered where she was off to, my old Miss Shiny – home to her des res to cook a roast dinner for her handsome husband and two-point-four children, probably, in her 4x4. The daydream was so vivid that I even saw myself standing up and grabbing my coat, tucking the binoculars into my bag, and leaving the office, entering the lift and descending to street level, and stepping out into —

Well, you catch my drift. I skipped along behind her as quietly as I could, not that she'd have heard me over the click-clack of her stilettos. She turned right into a quieter street, reached her 4x4 and … walked straight by it, instead slipping her key into Nissan Micra that had seen better days.

Shelley Patterson? Driving a '05 Micra? Hello Karma, my old friend. Off she roared, driving it like she'd just stolen it and spluttering the kind of smoke a stage school would have been proud of. Wouldn't *you* have jumped into a taxi and said, 'Follow that car!'?

The Micra zig-zagged its way down to the coast road, creeping south past the high-rise apartments and out into suburbia. The meter was moving faster than my taxi, so I was relieved when it came to a sudden stop outside a row of shabby two-storey houses – council houses, I believe they're called. There was a peace sign on one of the doors that had probably been graffitied there in the '60s, but she walked past that one and on to the end of the street, where a new-build apartment block reared up into the sky. One of those radical kind of apartment blocks, where the whole building seems to be glass, with a different movie playing behind every window. Here a couple cooking, there some kids watching TV, families either unaware they were visible or uncaring. Or maybe, having invested every last penny in their concrete box, there was no money left over for curtains and blinds.

The taxi driver said he didn't mind waiting but he'd have to charge extra if I planned on using his car as a viewing platform. So I put away the binoculars and paid him, and strolled across the road to the bus stop across the way. Behind me waves crashed against the rocks, sending spray in over the shelter. The street light was broken, which was both dangerous and handy. With my hood pulled up, there was little chance that Shelley would recognise me if she glanced out. Then again, she'd never noticed me before. Why should she start now?

***

I'd never wanted to give up. Something always made me hold on. Eventually the self-belief came, but in the beginning I felt torn from the shore, drifting on my raft and lost and alone forever, providing you didn't count the woodlice.

We were displaced into high society by a benevolent cousin of Mum's. Shotputted into the Southside from a dingy flat across town. The hand up felt like a slap back. I never fitted in, no matter how hard I tried. We never had a place in Brittas Bay, or two cars – or even one car, for that matter. Still, I always had my conviction. A belief that someday I would grow up and tear free from the misery. When I could be me, whatever that would be. Through the turbulent teens I held on, morphing into a quirky, strong-willed girl with a strong will.

And then I met Ugly Annie.

It was a school day just like any other. I dressed and fed Anthony, wrapped his hand in mine and wandered towards his school. Protecting him from guard dogs, with a cool sea breeze in our faces, I was someone: a big sister, a person in charge, a girl who mattered. Half an hour later I was surrounded in my classroom. Chanting, name-calling and the usual jibes.

On reflection, I'm pretty sure I *did* smell. Our ancient and freezing bathroom didn't lend itself to lingering visits. But it was more than that. It was our creepy three-storey house with its blanket of ivy. Mum's old-fashioned bicycle certainly didn't help.

Our school was situated in a refurbished old house by the sea in the heart of Dublin's trendy Southside. The village wasn't especially upmarket back then, though. Just a little fishing village with a bookshop, a toy shop, a health centre, a mini-market, a couple of butchers and lots of pubs.

There were no coffee shops but there was a sweet shop and every day after school most of the girls went there. I lived in the other direction, so I had no excuse to pop in. My way back home was long high walls, guard dogs and a cutting sea breeze. Shelly, on the other hand, would always head off home through the main gates. She would stroll down to the sweet shop flanked by her supporters, all of them with their socks down to their ankles, rebelling in their own tiny way.

That day I left by the back lane, the servants' entrance so to speak, passing the tennis courts and hockey pitch on my way and taking the long lonely road home. I was glad of the peace, actually, as it had been a long day. Except that Shelly had had no sweet money. No Curly Wurly for Shelley, so she'd decided to take the slow way home. As I turned into the lane she appeared before me, smirking and sneering. I stepped back and stumbled over her sidekick, whose leg just happened to be sticking out. Down I went onto the soggy, disgusting leaves. No one reached to help me up. Instead they circled around, chanting and laughing: 'Ugly Annie, Ugly Annie!' they bellowed as I scrabbled for footing and tried to stand. But my school bag was weighing me down and they left me no space, so there I squatted until they got bored and wandered off, still chanting, leaving me alone, cold and hurt, and with some very important small thing inside broken forever.

***

Facebook tells me that their clique is still intact. All the Ms Shinys, all plucked and perfect, not a hair out of place. They can frequently be found sipping wine at sunset looking out over Dublin Bay. Their homes are spotless and squeaky-clean, all courtesy of Tatiana and her bi-weekly dust-and-sweep.

I hope I am not coming across as bitter. They did me a favour, really. I know who I am, and what I do not want. Who I do not want to be.

And yet here I am, dusk coming on, huddled under a lonely bus stop in the rain, binoculars raking the apartment building across the way for a clue as to why Shiny Shelley is haunting bookies these days …

There! A second floor apartment, even more brightly lit than the rest, a mustard couch so vividly coloured that must be visible from space, and the only colour brighter is that of the red three-inch stilettos. She's stretched out on the couch now, hiking up her skirt to reveal the kind of fishnet tights that might have been considered erotic in the decade before she was born. Moments later an older man, slightly hunched and very ugly, crawls into view. In no time at all he's stroking the fishnets, then lowering his head to her feet. Is he *licking* the stilettos? A sickly feeling swims through my stomach, a mixture of guilt and glee. This is even better than I could have hoped. Now comes rapid flashes of light, and I realise that there is a photographer somewhere in the room capturing Shelley's finest moment for posterity. Joy!

And then … a bus. And then another one, right behind. Typical. You wait for ages hoping no bus will come along, and then there's two. When the second bus departs it takes a couple of seconds to refocus the binoculars, to find the right apartment window, but it's too late. The curtains are still open but the lights have been turned off. Are they finished? Did they somehow twig to my Peeping Tom act? Either way, my work is done here. I head off, aiming for the next bus stop. Back in town I hop off at the Lido takeaway on Pearse Street and celebrate with a sloppy chicken burger and chips.

And, need it be said, a glass or two of the stuff that cheers. When I wake the next morning, before the alarm, it takes a second or two before I remember my Facebook odyssey the night before, trawling through Shelley's life as she moved from one cocktail bar to another, living out in Fancyville and driving a BMW saloon. And no, she doesn't have an identical twin who runs around having her stilettos licked.

And I remember, too, realising that Shelley might be a fake and a fraud, but that she'd earned that BMW saloon the hard way. Few people are brave enough to try on the red three-inch stilettos, but Shelley certainly walked the talk. Ugly Annie had been at my elbow last night, urging me on, daring me to leave an anonymous comment or two – 'Nice shoes, Shelley. You can't lick good shoes!' – but in the end I declined. Karma's a bitch, and so was Shelly Patterson. They're welcome to one another.